Yucatán's Magic – Mérida Side Trips

Treasures of Mayab

By John M. Grimsrud

Edited by Jane A. Grimsrud

Contents

Introduction

Yucatán's Magic - Mérida Side Trips looks beyond the obvious popular tourist attractions, the luxury coast resorts, and the modern conveniences of big cities to discover the unique Yucatán.

From the Puuc hills to the extensive coast of Yucatán there are thousands of kilometers of paved quiet roads through countless Mayan villages interspersed with colonial haciendas and ancient Mayan ruins, all there just waiting for your visit.

This is photo-op and bird watching country that is the very finest this planet has to offer.

Over a quarter of a century of inspired exploration and recording of our travels while living in Mérida, Yucatán, has led to an impressive collection of outings that are the foundation for this book, built one story at a time. We present the best of the best.

Over the years we have enjoyed driving, busing and cycling this unique end of the world with its year round tropical weather.

Get off the main roads and away from the trendy tourist attractions to discover the hidden places (gems) of the real Yucatán. After all the point of this is to have as much fun and pleasure as possible.

Mystical magical Yucatán is the tropical gem of the planet. This semiarid tropical peninsula consists of three states, Campeche, Yucatán, and Quintana Roo. It is surrounded to the north and west by the Gulf of Mexico with balmy beaches and lagoons abounding with flamingos, and to the east is the Caribbean Sea with miles of sandy beaches, plus one of the world's largest coral reefs.

To the south lies the almost endless expanse of the Petén jungle, a nearly impenetrably lush rain forest isolating and preserving the sanctity of countless mysterious Mayan metropolises of that once flourishing civilization.

This book contains our favorite travel adventure trips of the places, excursions and outings, which we like for different reasons. Among them; tranquility, history, a view of quaint villages, a connection with the ancient Maya, changing scenery, and a look at another aspect of life that will take you out of the mainstream and off the beaten path.

This isn't a guide book but an idea book. It is something of another element to give you direction with your guide books like Lonely Planet or Moon Guide.

This book is not made to compete with guidebooks—it is made to complement them.

It is essential that you get a copy of the Yucatan Today magazine for their good maps and helpful travel tips. It is free and available at most restaurants and hotels in Mérida.

Many of our excursions have been by bicycle and bus. Bicycle and bus excursions in Yucatán are by far the most inexpensive you will ever take and can be the most rewarding in not only health benefits but also in memorable experiences.

In a small village some young Mayan girls ran after our bicycles and stopped us. They said that they were learning English in school and wanted to practice. One girl said; "I am sure that you find our country strange and interesting, and if I went to your country I am sure that I would find it strange and interesting too."

For the armchair traveler and people that have been to Yucatán before and think that they have done everything, *Yucatán's Magic – Mérida Side Trips* will open the door to another side of life not presented in tours or guided excursions.

We invite you to step into this different dimension and build your memories in the manner the Mayas built their pyramids, one piece at a time.

John M. Grimsrud

Chapter 1

Mayapán–Acanceh

Visit the Land of the Maya, Past and Present

These two unique and seldom visited archaeological sites are interesting, very memorable, and they are close to Mérida. This easy and convenient bus day trip is one of our all-time favorites.

What makes these two places so great is the fact that they can both be visited in an easy day trip out of Mérida by bus. Local transportation is readily available.

Start early from the Noreste bus terminal on Calle 67 and Calle 50 for the 47 km. outing.

Buy your bus ticket to the Mayapán Archaeological Zone located south of Mérida, and the bus driver will let you off at the entrance to this seldom visited remote and tranquil Mayan site.

Plan to arrive at Mayapán before 9 a.m. on weekdays, and more than likely you will be the only visitors; it is well worth the effort.

Arriving at the entrance to quiet and pristine Mayapán in the early morning, Jane and I were treated to a very special reward of having this enchanted world of ancient Mayan heritage to ourselves.

Yes, we were happy to be there on a tropical morning and share a priceless memory making moment. The tranquility spoke to us with powerful vibes of the mighty Mayan empire that flourished at this very place.

Mayapán beckoned us to enter.

Mayapán is a monumental complex of over four thousand individual ancient Mayan buildings covering four square kilometers.

Mayapán is of significant historical importance. This was among the last big Mayan developments thriving in Yucatán before the arrival of the Spanish. Over 12,000 people lived here. It was founded about A.D. 1000 and was part of an alliance with Chichén Itzá and Uxmal. Mayapán emerged as the sole ruler of the region, but was ultimately overthrown. A revolt was organized about 1440, and the ruling family was killed, Mayapán was sacked, burned, and abandoned.

We first visited Mayapán more than twenty years ago when it was overgrown with tropical vegetation that was pulling down and destroying these beautiful creations of the ancient Mayan times. The subsequent restoration and preservation work that has been done is a remarkable success. Majestic beauty still abounds and speaks out from across countless centuries directly to us. Mayapán's architecture is comparable to Chichén Itzá but on a slightly smaller scale.

Mayapán ruins. On the left is the observatory.
The significance of the unique building layout at Mayapán is difficult to comprehend. Advanced minds proficient in mathematics, astronomy, and natural medicine created this colossal metropolitan center with an engineered purpose.

Four hundred plus years ago, while in its prime, these structures were all ornately plastered, painted, and decorated.

No motorized apparatus was accessible or sophisticated survey gadgetry was available to these craftsmen and engineers that erected these geometrically accurate edifices.

Today very little of the detailed plaster and frescos remain that adorned the structures. Unearthed at Mayapán were several ornate plastered glyphs that have now been restored.

John L. Stephens, in his book *Incidents of Travel in Yucatan* describes his visit to Mayapán in the 1840's.

"The ruins of Mayapán cover a great plain, which was at that time so overgrown that hardly any object was visible until we were close upon it, and the undergrowth was so thick that it was difficult to work our way through it. Ours was the first visit to examine these ruins. For ages they had been unnoticed, almost unknown, and left to struggle with rank tropical vegetation; and the major domo, who lived on the principal hacienda, and not seen them for twenty-three years, was more familiar with them than any other person we could find. He told us that within a circumference of three miles, ruins were found, and that a strong wall once encompassed the city, the remains of which might still be traced through the woods."

Mayapán, like almost all the other Mayan ruins, has been plundered and pillaged for the past four plus centuries. I find it most incredible that any ornate work still remains on site.

From the top of the largest pyramid, the Yucatán jungle still appears much as it did to John Stephens in the 1840s.

After your visit to Mayapán, walk 200 meters out to the highway and catch the first bus or taxi-van headed north back toward Mérida, and get off at Acanceh.

This story continues at Acanceh.

Acanceh, whose name in Yucatec Maya means cry of the deer, has a population of 14,312. It is a colonial city that has been continuously occupied by the Maya for centuries.

Acanceh sprung up around the remains of ancient Mayan pyramids, and it has restored temples in the center of the town and several others still standing throughout the area.

Acanceh's central plaza with an ancient Mayan pyramid.

On Acanceh's plaza is located a colonial church, Mayan pyramids, and a municipal market.

The market is busy and crowded in the mornings. At midday the market place slows its pace. Afternoons are for lunch followed by a siesta. The siesta is enjoyed swinging in a hammock while waiting for the hot afternoon sun to sink low and ease the heat of the tropical day.

At the Acanceh market, the Mayan staff of life, the corn (*maiz*) tortilla, is sold by the kilo, hot and ready to eat.

All across Yucatán, tortilla shops, known locally as *tortillarias* or *molinos,* can be found busily producing stacks of tortillas. Tortillas are sold by the kilo or even the gram. These shops emit a distinctive roaring sound that alerts us so we can then follow our ears directly to the tortilla shop. We feel that our adventure tours are not complete without the purchase of at least 250 grams (¼ kilo) that we traditionally love to snack on lightly sprinkled with salt, rolled up, and savored at our coffee break time. At home we dry and roast tortillas to make our own *tostadas*.

The Mayan tortillas are made of corn. More than three thousand years ago, the ancient Maya discovered a process where the raw corn is boiled with powdered lime and then soaked overnight to release the corn's nutrient qualities. This process, known as nixtamalization, is credited with enhancing their diet to the extent that the Olmec, the ancestors of the Maya, were in the position to develop their advanced civilization.

We jokingly say that the Yucatecan food is so good and plentiful that it could easily get you resembling a short stack of tortillas.

Religious procession in Acanceh, and the ancient Mayan pyramid in the center of town.

The conquistadors didn't manage to take down all of the Mayan pyramids by quarrying them for their stone in a zealous quest to erect communities and churches.

The pyramid situated on the town central plaza of Acanceh somehow partially escaped that fate. Judging from the Spanish Inquisition colonial period construction, many Mayan structures had to have fallen prey to the pirating of their stone. Though the Spaniards efforts met with huge successes across Mexico judging by the tremendous number of cathedrals, they didn't have 100% success.

An ideal way to tour Acanceh is to hire a tricycle taxi. The cost is very affordable.

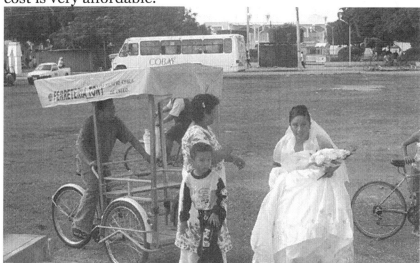

This beautifully bedecked young bride arrived at the church on her wedding day in a tricycle taxi.

We hired a tricycle taxi and traversed side streets on our way to visit a second Mayan pyramid several blocks from the city center. Young and old, walkers and riders fill all the little streets on market mornings and make the ancient Mayan town vibrate with life.

Before returning to Mérida, we stuffed ourselves on the generous portions of traditional cooking at a *cocina económica*. This restaurant is located adjacent to the bus terminal on the central plaza where buses and *colectivo* taxis depart for Mérida every few minutes. The superb bus service makes Acanceh an easy place to visit from Mérida. Even if you just bus over for a partial day tour and rent one of the many tricycle taxis to take in the city sights, visit the market, church, and ruins, and have lunch, you will pack in some very lovely memories.

This is the bus we arrived on, but we returned to Mérida in a *colectivo* taxi, which is much quicker but not as scenic a trip as the bus. In the background behind the bus is the *cocina económica* that we enjoyed so much and have visited often.

Towns nearby to the Mayapán Archaeological Zone and Acanceh that are well worth a visit: Tecoh, Cuzamá, Pixya, Telchaquillo and Xcanchakan. See chapters 8, 15, and 16.

Getting there:
Noreste Bus Terminal – Mérida
Calle 67 between Calle 50 and 52

MÉRIDA ↑ North;
All distances are to Mérida

■Acanceh 21 km

■ Tecoh

■Xcanchakan   ■Telchaquillo

↘Mayapan Mayan ruins 47 km
Mérida to Acanceh = 21 km, Mérida to Mayapan = 47 km

Chapter 2

Chumayel, Teabo, Maní, and Oxkutzcab

You may travel the world over and never find a stranger or more interesting adventuresome getaway.

After twenty-five years of exploring the back country of Yucatán, we find new quests are still abounding here in the real Mexico that tourists miss most.

This route was the key that unlocked the door to these rarely visited out of the tourist loop places.

We boarded a second class bus from Mérida bound for Chumayel with our folding bicycles stowed below. For two hours we sat back and were whisked along the seldom traveled back roads of Yucatán witnessing the quiet and quaint Mayan villages unaffected by the passing centuries.

(Bus departure terminals can be found in Chapter 19.)

We invite you to come along with us and share this infrequently visited magical paradise.

Chumayel

Chumayel is clean, quiet, and quaint and is known for the fact that the rare book of *Chilam Balam of Chumayel* was found here. This Mayan *codice* is a late 18th century manuscript copy of a Yucatec Maya chronicle. The text records the Spanish conquest of the Yucatán and provides much valuable information about the pre-Hispanic Maya.

The small village of Chumayel is situated in a typical Yucatecan countryside interspersed with centuries old haciendas and ancient Mayan ruins. The temple of La Purísima Concepción constructed in the 16th century stands at the center of the town.

Spanish influence here dates from before 1557. This was one of a hand full of churches of Yucatán designated on an ancient Franciscan map. Little has changed here over the centuries in Chumayel except for the coming of electricity and paved roads. It is a biker's paradise with a conspicuous lack of traffic. Our little Dahon folding bicycles make this type of road trip a joyful experience.

John in front of the temple of La Purísima Concepción.

Chumayel's meat market.

In the market of Chumayel, the meat is not refrigerated, but it is indeed fresh. When the meat hanging in the shop is depleted, business is concluded for the day. Tomorrow's supply of meat is tethered live to the pole in front of the market. In many small towns across Yucatán this type of meat market is a common sight.

Chumayel is too small for a regular market or even a business district but serenity is one of its attributes. Hourly bus service links north to Mérida and south to Oxkutzcab.

After consuming our breakfast and chatting with some Chumayel residents in the plaza area, we were on our bikes headed for our next destination of Teabo.

Teabo

Just four peaceful kilometers or one *legua* down the road, we arrive at the outskirts of Teabo. Teabo is relatively metropolitan compared to its rural neighbors.

After biking in the bustling neurotic traffic of Mérida, these lovely country roads where chirping birds and the wind in your ears are the only sounds, you mind is soothed, and the fresh flower scented air makes you want to drink it all in.

In the beautiful central park of Teabo.

We feel extremely fortunate to have such a wonderful ecologically friendly and healthy environment so accessible to Mérida. These lovely bicycle places are but a short scenic bus ride away. With our folding bicycles one of the nicest things of all is at a moment's notice we can change direction and be home from nearly anyplace in Yucatán in about two hours or less.

The tropical climate is another positive consideration which we happen to love. We do however try to do our cycling before the midday heat.

Another plus from November until March is that cold fronts will come through and hold the daytime high temperatures down in the low 20°C or 70°'s F—ideal for cycling.

Teabo church.

The vintage 1696 Franciscan colonial church stands at one end of the quiet central plaza of Teabo. This church is a gem to behold with its magnificently restored gilded altar and *retablos,* plus recently discovered rare 17th century murals, monastery gardens, and an interesting walled cemetery.

Teabo was originally an ancient Mayan settlement. Vestiges of the Mayan temples are still very evident on the church grounds and nearby. One of the colossal temples is still providing building materials for area construction centuries after the Spanish conquistadors began their occupation.

Within the Teabo church, restoration has been superbly done by the government agency INAH. Wall painted frescoes, altar pieces and *retablos* are brought back to their original state of splendor.

A feverish building frenzy saw this area explode with church construction and here in 1650 the Teabo church was begun; a project that would consume nearly half a century.

I will not try to give all the details here or explain the history because it is too involved for this story. However, I do recommend for those of you interested in learning more that you purchase and read the splendid field guide *Mayan Missions* by Richard and Rosalind Perry.

***Retablo* of Las Animas in Teabo, Yucatán.**

The Teabo church has some of the finest *retablos* in all of Yucatán. Truly incredible, the *retablos* and altar of Teabo have not only survived all these centuries but also the protracted Caste War and the Revolutionary War of 1910.

You will definitely want to take a close up look at this fine workmanship. It has weighty historical significance linked to the first European expression of Old World art forms found here in the Americas.

On the church complex grounds you can clearly see the various stages of restoration work being done.

In the quiet streets of Teabo, bicycles and tricycles are the principal forms of transportation.

Tricycles and bicycles on the streets of Teabo.

The *triciclo de carga* is used not only for freight but also employed as taxis. They become mini restaurants and purveyors of anything that can be sold on the streets.

Throughout Yucatán you will find many ingenious variations of these tricycles. Treat yourself to an experience of a lifetime and hire one of these taxis for a guided tour. This is something you can do nearly anywhere in Yucatán.

Tipikal
Seven quiet kilometers down the road is Tipikal, the next stop of our adventure.

Today this serene little settlement has nearly no business. These people are however self-sufficient, producing enough from their small *milpa* farms to feed their families but have nothing for export.

Church of Magdalena in Tipikal.

Poor to the point of poverty, Tipikal has no extra cash for frivolities like restoration.

Amazingly their stark church has stood here since its completion in 1742, and its condition is remarkably well preserved. The entry gate is of a similar style to those found at the old colonial haciendas across Yucatán.

Tipikal, Yucatán.

Thirty years ago when Jane and I first arrived in Yucatán over half of the homes outside of Mérida were *palapas*. The *palapa* was standard home construction for the Maya because all of the materials were available from the land. To this day you will find depictions of these homes carved in stone at area Mayan ruins like Uxmal, thus dating their use back thousands of years.

Five more kilometers down the road took us to the ancient and historical village of Maní.

Maní

Church of the San Miguel Arcángel, Maní.

The massive church and convent of Maní are built upon the site of a former Mayan temple and little has changed here in 450 years.

Maní is a small and tranquil Mayan village 80 kilometers south southeast of Mérida. Nearby is the shoe and pottery manufacturing city of Ticul, plus the garden market capital of Yucatán, Oxkutzcab, with good food and ample accommodations.

Maní is also situated on the age-old seldom traveled but famous *Ruta de Los Conventos* (convent route).

This seemingly unpretentious settlement has the incredible distinction of being continuously inhabited for the past 4,000 years by the Maya, one of the most technically advanced civilizations the world had ever known. But Maní's claim to fame is that following the Spanish conquest of Yucatán, Maní was chosen as the site for the first Franciscan mission in the region, and it is where the Franciscan Fray Diego de Landa burned the Mayan books and their religious artifacts while brutally torturing his victims in the courtyard of the former convent *San Miguel Arcángel*.

To further plunder these overrun indigenous, in 1562 Fray Diego de Landa burned and destroyed 5,000 Mayan figures of their gods, 13 altars, 27 parchment books made of deer hide and 197 decorated pottery containers of worship.

All of this was done to drive these "heartless heathens" to Christianity.

Today minute and modest Maní is serenely passive and it is hard to imagine that this off-the-highway rural community was once the tragic site of one of the most heinous degradations of cultural heritage and spiritual annihilation that this world has ever witnessed.

This is a look at the older side of Maní with a *palapa* home that is quickly becoming a thing of the past.

The massive church walls are the repository for the stones that formerly comprised the Mayan temple that originally stood upon this very spot.

Jane and I spent philosophical moments here contemplating this ancient convent and church and conversing about the haunting events that took place within these walls.

The church complex contains many artworks. When the history and significance of these works are known, the trip to Maní to witness them first hand becomes an imperative. Behind the impeccably kept *retablos* are located painted frescos that date back to the church's early days. They have been preserved and recorded by INAH, a Mexican governmental agency.

Main altar in the church in Maní.

These priceless treasures span the centuries with historical significance.

The gilded main altar is unequaled in any Mexican art work of the period and above it is an example of the fabulous fresco paintings that adorned the entire church at one time.

Take a close look at the intricate detail that adorns these significant *retablos* each conveying a momentous story.

The Maní municipal building, across from the church, was also built from stone salvaged from the ancient Mayan temple. It features Spanish colonial arches, with exposed wooden *vigas* or ceiling rafters.

A large painting hanging in the municipal building corridor depicts the *Auto de Fe* of 1562 when the sacred works of the Maya were destroyed. Also in that same corridor is a display of recent photos depicting Mayan ceremonies to their rain god Chaac. The area Maya still cling to and practice their ancient rituals.

A Mayan woman preparing *puchero* over a wood fire.

In an open air kitchen on the southwest corner of the central plaza a woman prepares *puchero* over an open fire across the street from the municipal building. *Puchero* is a traditional thick meaty soup with lots of vegetables. This lunch is for the school children and is dispensed for two pesos per person.

The Principe Tutul Xiu restaurant in Maní is popular with Yucatecan and foreign tourists. It is owned by the Xiu family who are descendents of the last Mayan rulers in the area. The restaurant features local favorites such as *poc chuc*.

Eleven kilometers more of biking, most were on a lovely bicycle path adorned by sculpted flowering bushes, and we reached our day's final destination of Oxkutzcab. Thirty-eight kilometers of quiet biking and exploring was enough for us. It felt good to check in to the Hotel Trujeque and take a refreshing shower.

Getting there:
Noreste Bus Terminal – Mérida
Calle 67 between Calle 50 and 52

Related chapters:
Chapter 3, Oxkutzcab

Side Trips:
The Maní area has excellent bus and taxi service to Mérida and Oxkutzcab with wonderful back road biking and side trips to Dzan, Teabo, Tipikal, Mamá, Oxkutzcab, Tekit, Ticul, and Tecoh.

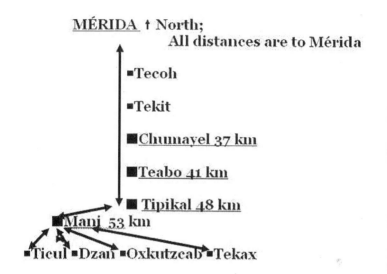

Chapter 3

Oxkutzcab

The place of ramon trees (ox), tobacco (kutz) and honey (cab)

Eighty kilometers south of Mérida is the Mayan city of Oxkutzcab. The name Oxkutzcab is of Yucatec Mayan origin and means in the place of ramon trees, tobacco, and honey, which are all products of the area.

Oxkutzcab is an intriguing market city that has excellent points of interest plus numerous fascinating adventures nearby. Things that you will want to do; visit the market and sample the exotic Mayan foods that change with the season, explore the recently restored 1693 Franciscan church...it is a beauty, take a people powered tricycle tour. Be sure to visit the hill-top hermitage chapel.

Side trips abound here. Visit the *grutas* Loltún (caves), Ruta Puuc Mayan ruins, the colonial towns of Maní, Dzan, Teabo, Tipikal, Mamá, Tekit, Ticul, Xul and Santa Elena. This is not an expensive place to visit. Accommodations are available from economy to moderate and eating establishments will entertain and feed you superbly.

Bus and taxi service in all directions is frequent. Some of the best bicycling is here.

Jane and I originally visited Oxkutzcab nearly thirty years ago when we ventured south out of Mérida on the narrow gauge railway train, one of the last operating in the world. That train has been out of service for more than twenty years now, and few people even remember it.

In those days Oxkutzcab was a frontier town with a vast jungle south that extended across the Puuc hills and off into Central America.

One thing that has hardly changed in all those years is that it is still a frontier. We were pleasantly surprised on this return trip. Even though the area has suffered somewhat from a lack of income due to many of its citizens being expelled from the U.S.A. where they had worked as undocumented workers, the city seemed to have gained a new invigorating attitude.

The returning workers brought with them money, new found skills, and a desire to make Oxkutzcab into their improved home. In what seemed to be a reversal of luck, these returning workers have made a positive change to Oxkutzcab.

So, come along with us and visit the new Oxkutzcab.

We spent the next two nights and days in Oxkutzcab indulging ourselves in a fun-filled fact finding tour rediscovering a town we thought we knew well.

***La Iglesia de San Francisco* in Oxkutzcab.**

First we look at the recently restored church, *La Iglesia de San Francisco,* located in the center of Oxkutzcab.

The restoration of the Church of San Francisco of Oxkutzcab was carried out in exquisite attention to detail by INAH, a federal governmental agency. This Franciscan church was begun in 1640 and finished in 1693 according to a stone plaque located over the front door.

The extraordinary transformation is evident and Oxkutzcab now has a real gem to be proud of. They even screened in the courtyard making the birds nest elsewhere.

Oxkutzcab is the market town for area produce. The market here bustles from pre-dawn until late night everyday of the week.

Colorful characters help make the Oxkutzcab market interesting and amusing. We met bushy haired Omar Antonio Bacalar (on the left in the above photo) several years ago when Jane and I took a bus trip far up into the Puuc hills to the little town of Yaxhachen. Omar, of Cuban origins, has amassed a considerable amount of notoriety from publicity he received since newspaper articles were written about his extensive natural medicinal cures, which he sells in his stall in the Oxkutzcab market.

Jane and I have discovered that downtown Oxkutzcab has become like a huge food court from early morning till late night. Some of the most interesting things of all are the continuously changing diversity of culinary options that await you.

Oxkutzcab's market still features the local Mayan specialty foods but the newly arrived workers returning from years of expertly gained knowledge in the U.S.A. have added a culinary flair.

Miguel Pacheco spent more than twenty years of his life as a chef in the U.S.A. He has brought back to Oxkutzcab Italian style culinary delights that have world class quality but Mexican prices.

Miguel's breakfast *burrito* creation that combined the very best of two worlds was not only savory but nutritious and sustaining.

Miguel made me happy. You can't beat a creative chef who loves to satisfy his clients.

Café la Cocina is located on the north side of the main market, and the tables are situated at curb side for pleasant people watching.

Morning, noon, and night purveyors of Mayan specialty foods that change with the seasonal crops arrive at the Oxkutzcab market and quickly sell out their inventory. Some of Yucatán's finest delights are only available at such places. Until you have partaken of these local favorites you haven't sampled the real Yucatán.

Tamales are a staple food throughout Mexico and are prepared in numerous different styles. One is called *torteado* and steam cooked within a banana leaf in which it is served. They are served topped with as much salsa as you like. Positively delicious!

Tamales served with a smile in the Oxkutzcab market.

Another style of tamale is referred to as *colado*. It has a lighter, fluffier, and thicker covering of masa or corn dough.

At the Oxkutzcab market most tamales are filled with chicken.

Tamales *horneado* are baked and can contain either pork or chicken.

Habanero hot sauce is an option with all tamales. You can use as much as you dare.

Mexico claims to have more than a thousand different varieties of tamales.

In Oxkutzcab, like all cities of Yucatán, tricycles are used for transporting anything that will fit in. This sign designates exclusive parking for these people powered freight haulers, here used as taxis.

Just one block removed from the main market, this typical old street of bygone years is a good example of colonial era buildings that still give Yucatán its old world charm.

Street vendors in Oxkutzcab sell the seasonal fresh fruits abundant in this area.

Oxkutzcab offers countless attractions and is a good start or finish point for visiting the Ruta Puuc. The Ruta Puuc or Puuc Route is a circuit of Mayan archaeology sites in the Puuc region. Puuc is the Mayan word for where the hills begin. The most important site in the region is Uxmal. The Ruta Puuc also includes the Loltún Caves located 5 kilometers up in the hills from Oxkutzcab. The caves contain paintings from the Mayan Late Classic period, and guided tours are conducted in both Spanish and English.

Getting there:
Noreste Bus Terminal–Mérida
Lus bus
Calle 67 between Calle 50 and 52
And
TAME Bus Terminal–Mérida
Mayab bus
Calle 69 between Calle 68 and 70
Or
Oxkutzcab Taxi Terminal – Mérida
Parque San Juan
Calle 69a between Calle 62 and 64

Hotel accommodations:
Hotel Puuc: 3 stars
Calle 54 and Calle 44

Hotel Ix Chel
Calle 53 No. 91-A between Calle 44 and 46
East of the main plaza. Clean budget hotel.

Hotel Loltún
Calle 53 between Calle 42 and 44
East of the main plaza. Clean budget hotel.

Hotel Trujeque: a budget hotel, clean with a prime location
on the main plaza downtown.

Related chapters:
Chapter 12, Yaxhachen – Oxkutzcab to Tekax

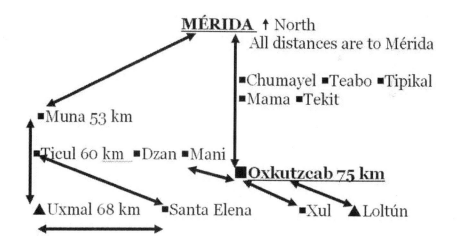

Chapter 4

Calkini, Becal, Halachó, Chuc Holoch and Nunkini

The old Spanish highway

Calkini is located seventy-five kilometers southwest of Mérida on the old Spanish highway known as *El Camino Real*, and half way to the city of Campeche.

Calkini, meaning in Maya power of the sun, was founded in 1549 by Franciscan Luis de Villalpando and has one of the few churches still occupied by the Franciscan order. The town grew rapidly and became the second largest city in Yucatán by 1588. The 16th century church of San Luis Obisbo is filled with interesting antique artifacts. The church has a remarkable long nave of 170 feet in length.

Prior to the Spanish conquistadors arrival here in 1549, little Calkini was a major hub of the *Canul* Maya with an enormous temple at its center. The *Canul* Maya emigrated from nearby Mayapán to the north in 1441 after that city was abandoned because of a civil war.

These *Canul* Maya were believed to have originated in the Peten jungle of Guatemala. They were mercenaries for one of the ruling families of Mayapán, the Cocom's, who were one of the last hold-outs against the Spanish conquistadors.

This is a very interesting and unique bicycling area that is definitely out of the tourist loop.

In order to best enjoy and get a good perspective of this matchless area, I recommend that you travel to Calkini by second class bus, which will take you on a two and a half hour scenic tour through the small off the main road Mayan villages along the way.

Catch this bus to Calkini at Mérida's TAME terminal located on Calle 69 between 68 and 70. You can return home on the rapid direct bus that makes it back to Mérida in about one hour.

Calkini is a clean and quiet town with nearly no motorized traffic and only two stop lights. The neatly kept central plaza and the city municipal building are perched upon the base of an ancient Mayan temple that also is the base for the adjacent huge church complex.

Church of San Luis Obisbo of Calkini on the left.

This new horse cart, the same as those used for centuries, has just returned from the jungle with a load of firewood (*leña*) and delivered it to a bakery (*panaderia*) in downtown Calkini.

Calkini is only 24 kilometers as the crow flies from Uxmal. Jane and I noticed a trail on our map leading in the direction of Uxmal. Always on the look out for a new road to bike, we set out to see if the route was passable.

In our quest for this bicycle route from Calkini through the jungle to the Mayan ruins of Uxmal, we encountered lovely Doña Ana who has lived on Calle 23 (the route to Uxmal) all her life. She is the caretaker of a small chapel on that same street a half kilometer from her home.

Our conversation with Doña Ana gets animated as she expounds about the wild jungle.

Doña Ana explained to Jane that a guide will be required for transiting the jungle/*milpa* trail to Uxmal and her brother might be available. Another word of caution was not to travel in the remote countryside with only two unarmed persons because it is too dangerous. A machete for snakes, and a mountain bike with fat puncture resistant tires and extra tubes are recommended.

Chapel in Calkini.

The reason you don't see any tourists in Calkini is because there are none.

We stayed at Hotel Milo, one of four hotels in Calkini. It was clean, airy, and bicycle friendly.

Calkini side trip – Bécal, Halachó, Chuc Holoch, Nunkini

Bécal, Campeche

Bécal in ancient Mayan times was the terminus of several *sacbe* roads. Later on the Spanish Royal Road (*El Camino Real*) linking the capital cities of Campeche and Mérida passed through Bécal. The ornate church dates from the 16th century.

Our first stop on our 40 kilometer Calkini area bike trip is in the little town of Bécal that is known for Panama hats made from a tender young palm leaf known as *jipi*. Other interesting novelties that include earrings of miniature Panama hats made of *jipi* are sold here. Twenty-five years ago Jane purchased a set of those little Panama hat earrings, which she has loved all these years, and now came back to renew them. Only young eyes can perform the intricate work of weaving these small items.

The ladies that weave these *jipi* objects do their work down in damp caves beneath the city where their materials will not dry out while being worked on. They invite visitors to watch them work, so come and take a look.

There are several shops selling Panama hats and other *jipi* trinkets in Bécal.

Bicycle traffic out numbers all other traffic in little Bécal. We cycled around town until we located the municipal market a couple of blocks off the main street and had our breakfast there. It was just ho-hum but we got fed, and for a town that doesn't cater to tourists, we felt lucky to find a selection of eateries in the market.

John in the main plaza of Bécal, Campeche.

The central plaza of Bécal proudly displays their claim to fame—giant sized Panama hats.

Crossing the border back into Yucatán on our five village loop trip, the departing sign says; "Campeche the hidden treasure of Mexico, we await your return."

Our next stop is the little town of Halachó, Yucatán, where they are having a street fair that takes over the downtown. There are few motor vehicles in town, and no one seems to be in a rush.

Halachó, Yucatán

Halachó has an exquisitely appointed church named *Santiago Matamoros,* which means literally St. James, the Moor slayer. The popular shrine of Santiago is famous for its equestrian statue of the saint.

***Santiago Matamoros*, St. James the Moor slayer, triumphantly in action with a dead or dying Moor beneath the feet of his gallant white steed.**

From Halachó our bike tour took us still further off the beaten path to Chuc Holoch, a strictly Mayan town of very friendly and inquisitive people who seldom see foreigners.

Chuc Holoch

When we arrived in town Mayan ladies were gathered with their homemade local foods for sale in a small park. The ladies in Chuc Holoch wear two distinctively different kinds of dresses. The traditional *huipil* is a white smock type dress richly adorned with hand embroidery and worn over a lace trimmed slip. It is worn by traditional Mayan ladies. The other ladies wear western style clothing and are considered *catrines,* women who have turned their backs on traditional Mayan or *mestiza* dress for *catrina* dress. The word *catrines* is used as an invective by elders in the village to express their disapproval of the women wearing modern clothing.

John with the Mayan ladies of Chuc Holoch.

Making tortillas in Chuc Holoch.

Our stop at a *molino* or tortilla shop in Chuc Holoch was almost worth the value of the whole trip because of the exquisite fresh ground, hot tortillas toasted to perfection that were as good as they ever get.

Jane and I have our ears tuned to the distinctive roaring sound of the burner that fires these automated tortilla bakers, and we instinctively purchase a quarter kilo to immediately eat. Lightly sprinkled with salt and rolled into a tube, they are part of the true taste of Yucatán. Out in the countryside it is common to get corn tortillas that are made of locally produced corn fresh from a real Mayan *milpa.*

Nunkini

Still out of the tourist loop, our next stop is at the appealing, quiet, and clean little town of Nunkini. Nunkini in Yucatec Maya means place where the sun is born.

The busiest intersection of Nunkini has a sleeping dog in the street and tricycle taxis waiting for customers under the shade of a giant *ceiba* tree—nobody is in a hurry.

Nunkini, like most towns in this part of the world, has street vendors selling home grown fruit, and often home cooked local items such as pork or chicken tacos or tamales wrapped in banana leaves.

If you have a peso or two you will always find something interesting and delicious to eat here.

The 17th century church is the focal point of numerous yearly festivals and carnival celebrations.

Small pox was unknown to this area until the 17th century when it struck with vengeance, taking many lives. People were mystified by the terrible deaths and one of the members of the community contacted a *curandero* "hmen" functioning as a clairvoyant. The "hmen" declared that the sickness came from white men and the only salvation was to make an effigy of a white man and burn it in a procession to the San Diego church.

When the Mayan community learned of this strategy to rid them of the small pox, all the people in area villages decided to make many white dolls. A celebration was made to the patron of Nunkini, San Diego de Alcalá; a great fire was made, the dolls consumed, and the anguish of the people turned to ashes. The small pox, like magic or a divine miracle, ceased.

Yearly Nunkini commemorates this event of Mayan mysticism commingled with Spanish Catholicism at a festival honoring San Diego de Alcalá. The festival concludes by the burning of white dolls. After the burning, the dolls' ashes are collected and mixed with water. Some believe that drinking this water can cure illnesses.

After the Revolution of 1910 in Mexico, the haciendas of the area were confiscated to the benefit of those who had suffered working from sun up to sundown in the fields of the plantations. A strong socialist movement began here in the early 1920's because many indigenous were still working in servitude.

Now many of the old haciendas have been restored and are used as hotels and centers for tourists while other haciendas remain as mute witnesses to an era of prosperity for a few and injustice to the Maya.

Prominently displayed in the center of the park of Nunkini is this exceptional work of art depicting a strikingly beautiful Mayan lady proudly holding the Mayan staff of life; corn.

After Nunkini, we completed our 40 kilometer circuit by returning to Calkini, ten kilometers away.

It is well worth the effort to find these isolated out-of-the-way places that make bicycle touring truly a joyous event.

Our hotel Milo was so quiet that we could hardly believe that we are still in Mexico, let alone the Yucatán.

In the morning we boarded the direct ATS bus back to Mérida, and we were there in about one hour.

After two nights and three action packed days, it seemed like we had been gone for three weeks.

This end of the world has more interesting adventuresome places to explore than you will be able to see in an active lifetime—so what are you waiting for?

Getting there:
TAME Bus Terminal – Mérida
Calle 69 between Calle 68 and 70

Hotel accommodations: At this writing at least four modest but clean hotels existed.
Hotel Milo is on the main street a few blocks from the main plaza. They are bicycle friendly, and they also have off-street car parking.

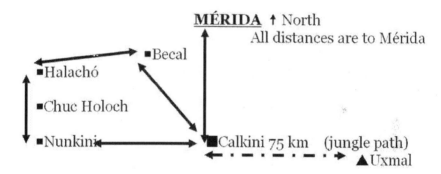

Chapter 5

Maxcanú–Oxkintok

The ancient Maya site of Oxkintok

Maxcanú, Yucatán, is in the western Puuc hill region with many *cenotes*, caves, and Mayan ruins nearby. Maxcanú is an early colonial city and was a front line of defense for the conquistador Spanish.

Jane and I departed Mérida by bus from the TAME bus terminal heading southwest 60 kilometers across the low flat semiarid scrub brush country to the colonial town of Maxcanú, Yucatán. It is situated on Highway 180 in the western most of the Puuc hills on the border of the neighboring state of Campeche.

This town that is seldom visited by tourists seems to be lost in a time warp far back in the past century. Maxcanú is one of countless Yucatán villages still maintaining the traditional thatched roof homes of the ancient Maya. A special tranquility is maintained in this place where bicycles and the three wheeled tricycle taxis quietly outnumber motor vehicles.

A side street in Maxcanú.

It is serene on the side streets of Maxcanú, but at the main plaza where we had our breakfast, resonating echoes barked out from an obnoxious ear-splitting brain-rattling megaphone that grated on our nerves with the repetitious tacky boom-boom-boom music interspersed with useless annoying advertisements. The main plaza was not a place we wished to linger.

We struck off on our bikes to get the general lay of the land, and to begin our photo-op country tour. Jane and I luckily found ourselves on the route to our end destination of the Mayan ruins of Oxkintok. Our map was not an accurate depiction of the roads. As it turned out, we were in luck because we did not have to go out on the main road to reach our destination— every day in Mexico is an adventure.

Oxkintok

Oxkintok is a seldom visited Mayan ruins off the main road. It is a lovely bicycle ride from nearby Maxcanú or Muna.

Oxkintok was made famous by author John L. Stephens on his epic journey of discovery in the early 1840s. He described the mysterious labyrinth concealed within the temple ruins.

The route took us on a back road through a *milpa* (cornfield) where we spotted a farmer cleaning squash (*calabasa)* to dry for the seeds. *Calabasa* is grown between rows of corn on the *milpa* farms.

This Mayan farmer is separating seeds from the squash.

From ancient times the Maya have sustained themselves with the perfect food group consisting of corn, beans, and *calabasa*.

This low impact farming is very labor intensive. The Maya employ slash and burn agriculture as their ancestors did over the past several thousand years. The farmers plant their *calabasa* at the beginning of the rainy season and harvest it in fall.

The seeds are collected, dried, shelled, roasted, and then used in the preparation of various local Mayan dishes. Our favorite is *Si Kil Pac*. This is a flavorful nutritious dish of ground squash seeds mixed with diced tomatoes, onions, chili habanero, sour orange, and cilantro. It is served cold and eaten with tortillas or tortilla chips.

We learned one interesting piece of wisdom from the *milpa* farmers. They told us that there was a big bank in town full of money but you couldn't eat the money. Even though their crop had little monetary value at 25 pesos per kilo, they could at least eat it.

Oxkintok.

Seldom visited and lightly excavated, the mysterious ruins of Oxkintok give haunting sensations of the Mayan civilization that flourished here for several thousand years.

Unique to this site are the many extensive inner chambers known as *El Laberinto* or the labyrinth, which were measured, explored and described by John Lloyd Stephens in his book *Incidents of Travel in Yucatán*.

The style of architecture is an interesting mix of Early, Late, and Terminal Classic techniques, and it is obvious that no standard form of construction is evident in these temples and pyramids. This was at the front lines of Mayan defense of their homeland and has not suffered the degradation of nearby towns where the Mayan temples were pulled down for conquistador expansionism.

We had this pristine end of the world to ourselves, a reward of an early start.

The only traffic we met on the road heading back to Maxcanú was on foot or bicycle. The man on the tricycle wears white long cotton clothing and sandals of the *campesino* or country farm worker of Yucatán. This was typical attire just a few years ago.

On our trip back to Maxcanú, we stopped to chat with the man that had been harvesting his *calabasa* seeds, and we could see the meager results of his morning's efforts in the white bag on the back of his bicycle. The production of the *milpa* farmer is hard fought for.

Back in Maxcanú we visited the colonial period church, cooled ourselves in the shade of the main plaza, which was now quiet, and planned our strategy for lunch.

The Franciscan church of San Miguel Maxcanú was erected in 1678. It is massive with a domed chapel and huge belfry. Its main *retablo* is of carved richly gilded filigree deep relief. It is from the baroque period. Bring your camera; this place is a real gem of pristine restoration and maintenance. A Mayan temple once stood on the site of the present church, but it is long forgotten.

Noon in the center of Maxcanú.

Lunch was next and *frijol con puerco* (black beans with pork) was the special of the day. It was tastily prepared and amply served at a reasonable market restaurant. The meal was served in a soup bowl filled to the brim with cubed pork, black beans, carrots, onions, and *camote* (a white yam). Side dishes of hot tortillas, hot chili *habanero* sauce, and a fried tomato sauce with quartered limes are included. Some places include the beverage, and you have your choice of a soft drink or something natural like lemonade, cool sweetened hibiscus tea called *jamaica* in Mexico, *horchata* (a sweetened rice drink) or other fruit juice depending upon the season.

A happy kitchen crew in Maxcanú produces a delightful dining experience.

No glitter and glitz, just honest good food brings in the hard working and hungry townsfolk.

This is the real Mexico that tourists miss most.

After our lunch, we loaded our bicycles into the luggage compartment of a bus that was headed to Mérida, and then we leaned back to dream a dream of our day's adventures while we rolled the 60 kilometers back home after thoroughly enjoying another fun-filled day trip.

Getting there:
TAME Bus Terminal
Calle 69, between Calle 68 and 70

Area points of interest:
Caves of Calcehtok, Oxkintok Mayan ruins, and Hacienda
Santa Rosa, a five star resort.

Bus and taxi service to Mérida and Campeche is frequent and
the area abounds in excellent quiet bicycling roads.

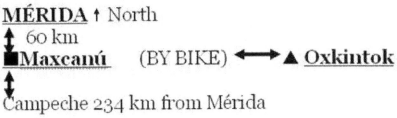

MÉRIDA ↑ North
↕ 60 km
▪Maxcanú   (BY BIKE) ←→▲ Oxkintok
↕
Campeche 234 km from Mérida

Chapter 6

Yaxcabá, Libre Unión, Tabi and Sotuta

A visit to the towns of the Cocom Maya and a one of a kind 18th century church

We packed a week's worth of activities into just one day.

A twenty minute bike ride from our home to the Noreste bus terminal in downtown Mérida is a joy with no traffic and a 21°C salubrious temperature.

At five a.m. the city streets were nearly deserted and quiet. Under a crystal clear high-pressure sky filled with stars, we ventured out onto the famous Paseo de Montejo. We headed south in the predawn. Cacophonous birds were chirping to a crescendo from their rookery trees that lined the avenue—a perfect start to a tropical January morning.

We were able to sizzle along with no stops and did not see traffic until we passed the downtown market that was already bustling with busy early morning business.

Our little 20 inch, seven speed Dahon folding bicycles make this type of trip possible and a real pleasure because the bikes roll fast and fold for stowage in just twelve seconds. They will then load into a bus, taxi or airplane.

Our second class bus took us on a very sinuous scenic small village route, off the main road.

At eight-thirty we were off-loading at Libre Unión, which is little more than a wide place in the road, some ninety kilometers east of Mérida.

Several taxi drivers met the bus and were competing for our business. We had already planned to use whatever type of transport we could to make the next leg of our trip. This was going to be a long action packed day even with the boost of a taxi ride to Yaxcabá.

We were lucky and got a flamboyant taxi driver who was bubbling over with local information.

On the road to Yaxcabá, over grown mounds, which are Mayan temple ruins, lined the way. One of the reasons that this area was so popular with the ancient Maya is that it is a zone of *cenotes* or sinkholes where water was available year-round.

Before 9 a.m. we were on the quiet colonial streets of Yaxcabá. Having our bicycles with us as ground transportation in these interesting out of the way places opens up exploration possibilities you would never get if you travel by automobile or are on foot.

We not only received a convenient ride from Libre Unión to Yaxcabá, but were informed and entertained all the way by our driver, Mario Briceño Dzul.

When we arrived in Yaxcabá, Mario topped off our enjoyable ride by singing a lovely ballad while passionately strumming his guitar.

Mario Briceño Dzul in Yaxcabá.

Although we found that there are many places to eat in Yaxcabá, we had packed along our breakfast, and we ate in the park while quietly watching the city doings.

We watched while a short of stature *campesino* (country man) lugged a large bundle of *leña* (firewood) on his back to cook his day's meals. The high price of cooking gas has forced many here in Yucatan to go to the woods for cooking fuel.

Quiet streets lined with picturesque colonial buildings and a magnificent 18th century church make this out of the tourist loop city well worth a visit for peace loving bicyclers.

San Pedro Yaxcabá.

The Yaxcabá church is a one-of-a-kind, like none other in Mexico. Inside the recently restored church, its splendor speaks out to you from over the centuries.

Nothing was spared in the restoration of the 1750's original *retablos* that now glisten with glittering gold leaf and meticulously painted deep relief carved figures.

Restored 1750s *retablo*, San Pedro Yaxcabá.

There are six exquisitely restored original side *retablos* in the church. You will definitely want to take the time to view these historical works of art that have survived trial and tribulation plus a protracted war that was at times centered in Yaxcabá. Also note the artistically painted original wall *frescos* that have survived nearly three centuries.

Over the years Yaxcabá has been a hotbed of armed conflict that fully exploded in 1848 during the protracted Caste War when 5,000 Mayan warriors burst into town. This was on the front lines of that prolonged conflict, and Yaxcabá was abandoned by its colonial defenders.

We leave Yaxcabá on this January morning headed into the tranquil back country.

Our next leg of the bicycle trip took us on a quiet rural road through *milpa* (cornfields) country to Tabí. This is a bird watchers paradise and bikers dream come true.

The name Tabí means in Yucatec Maya, the place where there are two *cenotes*.

Tabí is a very quiet Mayan village between Yaxcabá and Sotuta. Our map showed a dirt road from Yaxcabá to Tabí though now it is paved.

Both Tabí and Sotuta are seldom visited places with no hotel accommodations and scarcely any eating establishments. However, you won't starve in Tabi, ask around and someone will prepare you something to eat.

The Franciscan church in Tabi is reputed to have one of the finest baroque *retablos* and altar pieces in Yucatán.

Tabí church.

Colonial murals and frescos, the most complete sequence in Yucatán, are still in remarkable condition in the Tabí church. Restoration work has preserved this monumental historical treasure.

Chapel of the Virgin of Tabí.

Tabí has two *cenotes* and one is behind a weathered little stone chapel in the city center. This cenote has a fanciful legend surrounding it. Legend has it that in the 1600's the Virgin rose up from the waters of the sacred *cenote* in statue form, and she was deposited in the little chapel there. Then the bells of the chapel began to ring by themselves. The Virgin of Tabí became the entity of a Mayan religious cult.

Doña Chula with her grandchildren.

Our Mérida neighbor's mother, Doña Chula, lives in Tabí. We visited with these friendly, trusting, and good natured people, who do not lock their homes and trust their children to roam the streets unescorted—something not done in the big city.

Inquisitive and smiling children of Tabí.

From Tabí we biked on a very peaceful country road with gentle rolling hills, and a significant lack of traffic. Behind Jane, on the left, is a little Mayan chapel of three crosses from one of the religious cults that formed during the protracted Caste War as a rebellion against the Spanish conquistadors and the Catholic Church.

Chapel at entrance to Sotuta.

On the street from Tabí to Sotuta is a little chapel, a relic of the past. This part of the country abounds in such strange curiosities that make for photo-ops.

Sotuta

Historical crossroads of the Mayan civilization.

Our first visit to little Sotuta had been nearly twenty-five years earlier at the end of the thriving henequen era when Sotuta was at the end of the still functional narrow gauge railroad line. In those days the town was renowned for being the stronghold for a dissident populist autonomous movement in Yucatán and even had one of the most powerful radio stations blasting out their independent egalitarian message. The Mexican military maintained a fortified barracks prominently placed on the main city plaza from the beginnings of the Caste War in 1847 that was not relinquished until 1998 when indigenous rights were at a proverbial boiling point. This heightened indigenous rights movement was brought about by the EZLN or the Zapatistas who squared off and took on the Federal government January 1, 1994, forcing their issue of human rights into international news.

Nachi Cocom and Sotuta are synonymous. The Cocom family of Sotuta was one part of the warring Mayan faction that fought against the Xiu family of nearby Maní for centuries after the collapse of their northern empire following a two hundred fifty year draught.

The Spanish conquistadors, after being totally driven out of the Yucatán peninsula in 1535, returned around 1540 with a new game plan of divide and conquer, and that was to exploit the deep division between the two warring Mayan tribes. This was enough of a tactic to allow the Spanish to get a foot-hold, and by 1542 they put down roots in T'ho, now known as Mérida.

This statue of Nachi Cocom is in the center of Sotuta.

The palace of Nachi Cocom

In the center of Sotuta stands a fortress looking building known as the palace of Nachi Cocom. The building now houses a museum and has an interesting but cloudy history. It is obvious that it stands upon a Mayan temple and the structure is constructed from materials taken from it. The dates of subsequent construction at this site are purely conjecture. It is likely that the famous Mayan king Nachi Cocom had a home here when the Spanish took Sotuta in 1542 and made a prisoner of him in 1549. The Spanish built a military barracks at this spot in the 18th century and it became an armed garrison in 1848, occupied until 1998.

17th century Franciscan church in Sotuta.

The Sotuta church began as a Franciscan mission with an open air thatched roof Indian chapel in the mid 1500s. By the 17th century the present church was completed. Four ornate gold leaf adorned *retablos* dating from 1550 to 1730 can be found in the Sotuta church.

Building on the Sotuta plaza.

In Sotuta, traditionally dressed Mayan ladies carry their ground corn home from the *molino* in the style of Yucatán, on their head. This corn is from their own local *milpa* farms.

El Goyo of Sotuta.

Friendly old "El Goyo" keeps the city plaza spotlessly tidied up. He showed us his treasured watch, a gift from his 45 year old son that immigrated to the U.S.A. and seldom returns to visit. Many local families are divided by this economic immigration.

Real wealth is found in the smiling faces of these otherwise economically depleted locals.

Tricycle taxis of Sotuta line up at the plaza.

In front of the municipal building non-polluting quiet tricycle taxis queue up for prospective customers. Across from the municipal building is located the *cocina económica* where we have lunch each time we revisit the area while waiting for the return bus to Mérida.

Our no frills lunch spot, Los Arcos, is housed in an ancient colonial building. The owner, Margarita Rejon, and her friend Mirna Cocom jovially entertain us with hilarious accounts of local happenings, and the food is good.

Cocom is a family name synonymous with nearly five centuries of Sotuta history.

In the central plaza is a stone bust of Nachi Cocom—still a legend.

Oriente bus terminal in Sotuta, Yucatán.
Our bike tour over, I loaded our bicycles aboard our bus back to Mérida, and I got a snooze along the way.

Getting there:
Noreste Bus Terminal – Mérida
Calle 67 between Calle 50 and 52
Oriente bus

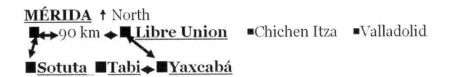

MÉRIDA ↑ North
■→90 km ◆■Libre Union ■Chichen Itza ■Valladolid
■Sotuta ■Tabi◆■Yaxcabá

Chapter 7

Izamal, to Kantunil with Visits to Cuauhtémoc, Sudzal, and Xanaba, plus a Side Trip to Kimbilá

One of the all time best one-day Yucatán getaway excursions we have found.

This is an easy and pleasurable trip. To maximize the pleasure of this adventure we recommend taking the Centro bus that departs at 6:45 a.m. from their terminal on Calle 65, two blocks east of the main market, adjacent to and east of the *Casa de Pueblo*.

There are faster ways to get to Izamal but this back road route, though slow, is a pleasant look at the Yucatán that most tourists miss.

Our bus route took us first east to Tixkokob, famous for its hammock makers. Being a local bus, we were steadily acquiring more and more passengers heading to the remote villages that lay ahead. As we passed our next town of Cacalchén, the road narrowed perceptibly, and each of the upcoming towns in turn grew smaller and smaller heading to Bokobá. Tekantó, Tixcochó, Teya, and Tepekán are all typical quiet and picturesque Mayan villages where many of the homes are *palapa* thatched huts situated among remnants of colonial era haciendas. At rural Tepekán we made our final turn, and we headed into Izamal on a road as straight as a die, and we knew that this roadway had to be a remnant of an ancient Maya *sacbe* road built countless centuries before.

Izamal

As tourist end destinations go, Izamal is one of Yucatán's finest, and well worth your time to explore and get to know.

Izamal, known as the yellow city because most of its buildings are painted yellow, is a lovely colonial town that contains gigantic Mayan temples throughout. Climb to the top of the tallest; the view is spectacular. Explore the magnificent 1500s church. Tour guides are available at the church and monastery entrance. Take a carriage ride or tricycle taxi city tour, visit the municipal market, and sample the local foods that range from fine dining to a *cocina económica* where you can get stuffed on local specialties at bargain prices. Souvenir shops abound and real authentic Mexican folk art is here.

Izamal was put on the modern map by a visit from Pope John Paul II in August of 1993. Bishop Fray Diego de Landa put it on the ancient map in the 1500s.

Statue of Bishop Diego de Landa in Izamal.

Izamal has a rich Mayan and conquistador history. Huge temple pyramids are still part of the town. A 16th century Franciscan monastery is situated atop the base of one of them. The statue in the photo above of Bishop Diego de Landa faces the monastery he directed to be built. In July

1562, Friar Diego de Landa held an *auto de fe* Inquisitional ceremony in Maní, burning a number of Maya books and 5000 idols, saying that they were "works of the devil."

Izamal is a major photo-op stop and tourist destination in Yucatán. I will not attempt to do justice to the many impressive Mayan pyramids or spectacular colonial structures.

The colossal amount of stone harvested from the ancient Mayan temples that stood here to build this city center is simply mind boggling considering that several enormous pyramids still remain standing to this day. We recommend Izamal as a must-see place. Bring your camera, read-up ahead of time, and by all means take a guided carriage ride.

Take your time and spend two or three unhurried days here. It is just too good to hurry through. *Calesa* horse drawn carriages are for hire as taxis or for city tours. We and our visiting friends have always found these easygoing carriage tours the highlight of the trip.

The Road to Kantunil

On this trip, we continued on our bikes south to Kantunil. We love the fresh air and quiet nature we found along this seldom traveled road.

Cuauhtémoc and Pixilá

Down the road south from Izamal we arrive at the small village of Cuauhtémoc where the ruined church of Pixilá stands upon the mound of a ruined Mayan temple.

Little Cuauhtémoc is rural and on the verge of being desolate. Time has silently passed by here with little notice.

The unhurried main street of Cuauhtémoc is where we can hear a car coming from kilometers away. The contrast to Mérida's push and shove commotion makes us want to whisper.

Church dedicated to the Virgin of Candelaria.

Some attempts at restoration and upkeep are visible at Pixilá's 18th century church which is dedicated to the Virgin of *Candelaria*. A plaque above the front door is inscribed; *Se acabo año* 1797 (work was finished in the year 1797).

Still roofless, the Pixilá church was originally built with a thatched roof. Amazingly the forlorn little old church is still in use. As we visit the hushed little village it is hard to imagine a time when enough eager souls diligently put forth the effort to construct this church. After more than two hundred years of deterioration someone is making attempts at restoration. This seems to be moving ahead at a pace similar to the rate that the mail is delivered in Mexico.

Continuing south down the quiet road with a tail wind, we arrive at silent and clean Sudzal. There is a beautifully pleasant overpowering aroma of orange blossoms filling the fresh country air, and it makes us want to drink it in. It is a shame we couldn't take a photo of the odiferous perfumed fragrance.

Sudzal has been a hamlet and regional part of Izamal since the 16th century. The Mayan name means a narrow place, and from the looks of the town, little of significance happens here in Sudzal giving it a very pleasant and tranquil atmosphere.

Sudzal's 16th century church has been renovated.

Sudzal is conspicuously devoid of visitors and traffic.

Other than some power poles, the vista around Sudzal has changed very little over the centuries. These gems of the past are becoming few and far between, but here along this road are several towns still missed by the hurried tourist crowd. It makes for a perfect bicycle day trip.

The Sudzal city building and church seem abandoned with little street traffic and just a few chickens and turkeys left to pluck unhurriedly along their way. Jane and I have found another slice of bike paradise.

Xanaba

Xanaba is barely a wide place in the road. The rural countryside is little disrupted by its presence.

This locality seems to be made to order for cross-country bikers like us who positively love the quiet pastoral countryside.

Xanaba church.

As minute and inconsequential as Xanaba was, the simple, clean and neat little church is the centerpiece of the town. Some people call Xanaba home though it is only on the road to somewhere else.

A surprise awaited us when we ventured south headed into our day trip's next stop of Kantunil.

A real bicycle obstacle course awaited us. Evidently the transportation department had taken little notice to the fact that bikers may want to pass between these two towns. Just before entering Kantunil, we encountered the new approach to the toll road; it was barricaded with a huge barrier accompanied by a no bicycles sign. We had to hoist our bikes over the obstacle, pass through the woods on a small walking path, and then ascend a high drainage curb in order to traverse the next two lanes of high-speed highway. We persisted and arrived at the outskirts of Kantunil.

Kantunil in Yucatec Maya means precious yellow stone. Kantunil is on the main road from Mérida to Valladolid. It has excellent bus and taxi service, a 16th century church with many ancient Mayan artifacts including musical instruments such as the *tunkul*, a Mayan log drum.

This little town had every appearance of being upscale. It is on the bus route to Mérida.

The lovely morning was made even better by connecting with the Mérida bound Oriente bus that arrived with perfect coordinated timing.

We stowed our folding bicycles below, climbed aboard in air conditioned comfort, and I didn't awaken from my profound snooze until we were rolling into the Mérida bus terminal.

After this outing we were able to scratch one more road trip off our list. As it nearly always happens when we remove one trip from the list, we add two more. Well, with this trip we added four new ones while we passed numerous side roads that need exploring.

Twenty five years of cycling around Yucatán and our bicycle adventure list continues to grow longer.

If we could find a better place we would be there.

So, stay tuned as we keep scratching bicycle adventure excursions off our ever expanding list.

Another option for a visit to Izamal.

Kimbilá and Citilcúm to Izamal

On a cool gray January day that Jane and I had anxiously been awaiting, we leisurely biked to the city center and boarded the Oriente bus to Kimbilá.

The Mérida to Izamal bus passes a number of classic colonial towns of scenic interest.

Church at Kimbilá.

We got off the bus in front of the church in the center of Kimbilá. Everything you will want to see and do in Kimbilá is within two and a half block radius of this well kept church.

Fresh cut meat is sold in the center of Kimbilá directly in front of the church. The open air meat market is a simple affair consisting of a few boards with meat hooks that hold the freshly butchered pork aloft above the serving counter. The inventory is quickly liquidated and the little market vanishes away in a tricycle that will return another day with freshly butchered and never refrigerated meat for vending.

Parking and traffic are not problems in Kimbilá where the scarceness of motorized vehicles and the absence of stop lights create a welcome relief from Mérida's pushy-shovey horn-honking madness.

Ten in the morning finds us having our morning iced coffee and fresh locally made hot tortillas on the main street of Kimbilá. It is so quiet we become anxious in anticipation of some unforeseen event that is surely not going to happen here anytime soon!

Jane had a reason for coming to Kimbilá.

The village of Kimbilá, with a population of 3,500, has been the center for the manufacture of typical Yucatecan clothing for more than 30 years. All the factories have outlet stores where they sell a big variety of items, including *guayaberas* (the traditional Yucatecan dress shirt), *huipil* (the traditional Mayan dresses), and blouses with a wide variety of embroidered patterns.

Jane shopped in some of the Kimbilá stores featuring the locally made handiwork of the talented sewing artisans.

After making our purchases in Kimbilá, we biked on to even smaller Citilcúm.

The town of Citilcúm on our way to Izamal is little more than a wide place in the road. Check out this main *zócalo* park directly across the street from the church. It is skinny pickings for this horse sniffing out a meager meal of dry parched nearly invisible grass.

Citilcúm; a truck hauling henequen to be processed into fiber.

Henequen cut and neatly stacked atop an antique truck rolls through town on its way to be processed into sisal rope fiber. This is becoming a rare sight in Yucatán these days. The process is so labor intensive that even Mexico is losing out to the cheaper producers like Brazil.

Across the street from the main plaza of Citilcúm is a 16th century church that originally started as a thatched roof affair and was completed in 1653.

This short excursion ends for us in Izamal, where we went in search of lunch.

The Izamal municipal market is a good place to look for food.

A couple of blocks east of the main square Jane and I found a lovely little *cocina económica* that produced a hardy local dish known as *potaje,* which is a stew heavily laden with vegetables, pork, lentils, and spiced just right. The option of adding lethally hot *habanero* sauce is at your own risk. Fresh tortillas are included with the meal. The portion is exceedingly sustaining and a required quantity for active bicyclers.

With our shopping bags and our stomachs full, we biked to the Izamal bus terminal, and we were soon aboard a bus heading for Mérida.

Getting there:
Terminal del Centro – Mérida
Calle 65 between Calle 46 and 48
next to the *Casa del Pueblo*

or

Noreste Bus Terminal
Calle 67 between Calle 50 and 52

Hotels:
Hotel Macan ché – Izamal
Bed and Breakfast
www.macanche.com

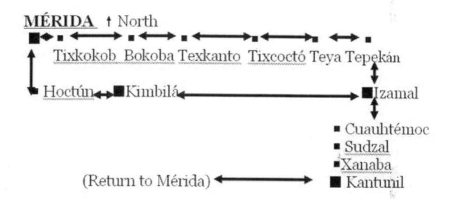

Chapter 8

Tecoh

The place of the puma

- •A day trip
- •A starting point for a trip to Tekit and Ticul
- •A starting point for a bicycle trip to Cuzamá
- •A stop between the Ruins of Mayapan and Acanceh

Tecoh, in Maya meaning the place of the puma, is a village on the highway between the colonial town of Acanceh and the Mayan ruins of Mayapán.

Tecoh has a number of interesting points of significance. The centerpiece of town is definitely the 1751 church perched upon the high base of a Mayan temple. The baroque structure measures 150 feet on its vaulted roof. A visit to the rooftop is possible. You should tip the caretaker for opening the spiral staircase for you. The church has richly ornamented and restored baroque *retablos,* plus a *tunkul* ceremonial drum that was used until recently. A lovely guided *gruta* and *cenote* tour is started just south of town a few blocks...follow the signs. Visit the local market. Bus and taxi service is frequent.

Tecoh–A Day Trip

Jane and I have been making a point to take at least one excursion of exploration in Yucatán each week by bus, bicycle and occasionally just bike or bus.

We looked at the map and decided that Maní, a Mayan village continuously inhabited for the past 4,000 years would be our next adventure.

We had the bus schedule and would take departure at 8:30 a.m. from the Noreste downtown terminal where the back country buses leave from.

A couple of friends wanted to join us. Jane and I were first to arrive and went to buy our tickets. Surprise! Our 8:30 bus to Maní wouldn't leave until 9:30.

Plan "B". Take the next bus out!

The decision was unanimously made with our adventuresome foursome, get our tickets and ride to the end of the line—wherever that might be.

At 8:10 a.m., Jane and I plus our traveling companions Maria and Thalia were rolling on a second class bus out of town with a destination of Tecoh.

Where in the world was Tecoh?

We got out our map to find out where our adventure bus would leave us.

What a pleasant surprise!

It turns out that Jane and I had passed through quaint little Tecoh countless times and always commented that this was a place we both had secretly desired to explore.

We bounced along through serene Mayan villages and past ancient haciendas picking up and discharging smiling friendly inhabitants of these neat rural communities filled with tweeting birds and flowering shade trees. We stepped off our bus in Tecoh on the south side of the *zócalo*. This was the end of the line, and it was 9:20 a.m. Our foursome instinctively meandered around over to the south side of the *zócalo* (main plaza), which was in the shadowy shade of the intense tropical sun, to plan our next move. This seemingly tranquil little town has a central plaza more than two blocks long with a church from early colonial times prominently placed upon the north side.

It was another pleasant Yucatán morning in this little charming gem called Tecoh that greeted us with its peaceful passive streets abounding with unrushed bicycles, tricycle taxis, and pedestrians.

Tecoh was literally a breath of fresh air with its conspicuous lack of motor traffic.

To merely say the place was serene would be a gross understatement. It was a step back into time long ago forgotten and passed over by the go-fast gas-guzzling yuppie class.

We had found a true treasure and a real jewel in Tecoh.

In the 1550s the Franciscans established a mission here with the large church completed in the 17th century. The *retablo* (sculpture rising behind the altar) that covers the east end of the church has recently been restored and is considered the most elaborate in Yucatán. The present church is sitting upon the remains of a gigantic former

Mayan temple in a seeming attempt to silence the gods of old that the indigenous Mayan so proudly cherished.

John approaching the majestic church at Tecoh.

The climb up the base of the ancient Mayan temple to the old colonial Spanish church still speaks volumes of the thousands of years of Mayan culture trumped by the conquistadors who have now ruled here for nearly 500 years.

More photo-ops abound from the top of the centuries old colonial church where there is a spectacular vista to behold.

Getting to the roof top was an adventure unto itself.

We first tipped the church custodian to unlock the access door, and our challenge began. We groped our way on hands and knees up the ancient crumbling spiral stairs in near total darkness knowing that ultimately we would have to descend by the same route. It was downright spooky, but we persisted, and in the end it was well worth the effort.

We had a view looking across the city park toward the municipal palace from the top of the old church at the little unrushed town of Tecoh. Five hundred years ago the view from this very spot would have been from the peak of a Mayan temple.

Jane and I are successfully atop the church at Tecoh and under powerful tropical Yucatán skies.

A thing that was conspicuous about Tecoh was its cleanliness in every detail. I can remember back some 30 years when Mérida was clean and quiet like Tecoh still is today.

The ambiance and sparklingly clean and clear air of Tecoh immediately purged our bodies and souls of Mérida's big-city hustle and bustle.

On the shady south side of the *zócalo* along with numerous small businesses is located the brightly and neatly painted two story municipal building.

We naturally strolled into the open arched foyer with its mirror polished ornately adorned French colonial floor tiles that dated back 150 years to when Maximilian was Emperor of Mexico.

It was a pleasant surprise to be the only tourists in town. Tecoh's townsfolk were happy and eager to greet us with friendly welcoming smiles.

We climbed the broad stairway of Tecoh's municipal building, and we were rewarded with a view from the balcony looking north across the *zócalo* to the old colonial church. The little colonial era town appears to be like a tiny magical allusion below us, moving peacefully and unhurriedly.

View of Tecoh from the balcony of the municipal building.

Maria Laur in front of the Tecoh market.

On the sidewalk near the market is the medicine man.

The medicine man has the eager attentive audience captivated and assures them that he will cure their ailments with his secret herbs and mystic potions.

Tecoh's bicycle busy streets have almost no obnoxious auto emissions.

We took a tricycle taxi to visit the Grutas de Tzabnah, which are two kilometers south of town. On the tour you get to see a series of underground caves and *cenotes*, some with rare blind white fish and eels, and then swim in the last *cenote*. A Mayan guide will accompany you and point out all the interesting features. The fee is reasonable.

This is the friendly open-air kitchen at our lunch stop after our tricycle taxi city tour.

At the restaurant known as a *cocina económica* where we had lunch, the cook ground hot chili peppers in a *molcajete* as she prepared lunch over a wood fire in the traditional style of the indigenous. Our meal was superb and the quantity generous.

My lunch cost a mere 25 pesos and generously appeased my ravenous hunger.

Our adventuresome group was on the way back to Mérida by 3 p.m. Although the second class local bus was a fun-filled experience, we opted for a quick return trip to Mérida aboard a speedy collective taxi that bypassed the quaint villages, cutting the ride time in half. We were heading home on a hot afternoon to where our hammocks beckoned.

Afternoons in Yucatán are made for hammocks.

History at a Glance – *Cenotes* and *Grutas*

Yucatán has a one-of-a-kind topography. Yucatán is where 65,000,000 years ago an event happened that drastically and forevermore altered life on this planet.

The meteorite that impacted the earth struck the Yucatán with such an impact it brought about an ice age so abruptly that dinosaurs became extinct.

This impact formed the Chicxulub Crater whose epicenter was thirty kilometers north of Mérida, and the after-splash of molten rock sent projectiles as far away as Belize and the Mexican state of Veracruz.

With that meteorite impact the Yucatán became a geographical rarity with no rivers, only *aguadas*, *cenotes* and *grutas*. These are essentially the same thing but with different exposure to the earth's surface.

Aguadas **are open ponds near the surface.**

Cenotes **are sunken open ponds or sinkholes in the limestone rock.**

Grutas **are subterranean caves containing ponds.**

Tecoh, a Starting Point on a Tour to Tekit and Ticul

Biking the Tranquil Quiet Mayan Back Roads of the *Gruta Ruta.*

This adventure starts at the Noreste bus terminal on Calle 67 and 50 in Mérida. Jane and I took a 7:20 a.m. bus to Tecoh with our folding bicycles stowed aboard to begin our two day off the beaten path excursion to bike the zone of *grutas* and *cenotes* that I refer to as the *Gruta Ruta.*

We invite you to visit this truly unique place like none other. It is close to Mérida geographically, but centuries removed culturally.

After unloading our bikes at the central plaza bus stop in Tecoh, we purchased some fruit in the market just across the plaza and then struck off to find the sign to our first destination of Sabacché.

Sabacché

Sabacché, a small ex-hacienda village, was abandoned to another era. The humble little village subsists on a hardscrabble minimalist agricultural economy and has about twenty families.

Sabacché is more than just quiet, there is virtually no motor vehicle activity and the only businesses in town consisted of a *molino* to grind corn and a small convenience store located in a Mayan thatched roof *palapa*. The people were more than just friendly. When I went to the *molino* to try and buy a few tortillas for a snack, I discovered that they only ground the corn to make dough (*masa*). I spoke to them in Maya, and the lady asked me if I was hungry. I replied that I was. Even though they had no tortillas at the *molino*, in a few minutes a little girl arrived in the park with tortillas and a big smile. We have always found that these wonderful people would freely share whatever they had.

While we ate our tortillas, free ranging turkeys came to visit, pleading for a morsel.

John and José Pech Ramirez in Sabacché.

José Pech Ramirez, a resident of Sabacché, saw us in the park and came over and struck up a conversation with us. He invited us to see the recently improved *cenote*, and soon we were off on our bikes to visit a *cenote*.

While José Pech was speaking to us in English, his associates gathered across the road to observe our activities. When they saw us leave with Jose, they all got on their bikes and tagged along.

Whilst we biked to see the *cenote* José gave us a tour rich in area history. He told about his grandmother, a Mayan medicine woman or *curandera* who is knowledgeable in the local traditional herbs and native plants. She is eager to share her years of knowledge with everyone. José invited us to his home for dinner, but we graciously declined because we still had more than 30 kilometers of biking ahead of us, and once we eat a big lunch, our bicycles just about refuse to move, and our hammocks beckon us to repose.

We did however visit the *cenote* with its new stairway leading down to the water. The dense jungle setting has a mystical aura of fresh scented flowering foliage and the exuberant sounds of wild birds. We arrived by way of an ancient Mayan *sacbe* road. Still in use and perhaps thousands of years old, the *sacbe* road gave us an eerie and haunting sensation while we passed the way of countless generations through the pristine jungle. This *cenote* was part of the adjacent area settlement that included the Mayan ruins of Mayapán. See Chapter 1, Mayapán–Acanceh for more on Mayapán.

After thanking José for the tour and bidding him goodbye, we continued on our way along the *Gruta Ruta* road to Tekit. Along our way we encountered the humblest of roadside chapels with a candle burning.

Road side chapel.

These *Gruta Ruta* roadside chapels have a distinctive Mayan significance and are closely tied to the Caste War cult that worshiped the Talking Cross and later became the Cult of the Holy Cross. This cult religion sprang up back in the 1850s at Chan Santa Cruz now known as Felipe Carrillo Puerto and inspired the Maya to persist. The Caste War and the Cult are covered in our book *Yucatan for Travelers – Side Trips: Valladolid to Tulum.*

This quiet little route is a real plus to us bikers who prefer the sound of the breeze in the trees and free birds singing. We find the Mayan Holy *Cross* cult chapels intriguing and stopped to examine several along our route.

Chapel of the Holy Cross.

Tekit

Tekit.

Tekit is a small town rich in Mayan tradition with a diminutive posada hotel and a good restaurant. Tekit is a lovely quiet bicycle ride from Tecoh. Local festivals tend to pack the town on weekends. Bus and taxi service to Mérida, Oxkutzcab, and Ticul is frequent.

We took our lodging at Tekit's finest accommodation where the only rooms for rent are at the no frills Posada Can Sacbc. Can Sacbe is a Mayan word that means road of snakes.

After a long and lovely day of bicycle excursion, we were delighted and richly rewarded with an ample eating extravaganza of roast pork and black beans done to perfection, and garnished with traditional sauces at a restaurant located just around the corner from our hotel.

Lupita is the owner of the restaurant on Tekit's plaza who prepared our delightful lunch. She is pictured here with her ninety year old mother who still radiates a special beauty.

The next morning we silently rolled out of quiet little out-of-the-way Tekit early when the first patrons began opening the market, and the last stars still glimmered overhead. On the next 30 kilometer leg of our bicycle excursion, we left the small rolling hills of the *Gruta Ruta* and entered an area of the grander Puuc hills that extend across the southern part of the state of Yucatán. With only the two very small towns of Mamá and Chapab along our way, we enjoyed the open country of fresh air and wildflowers with dazzling iridescent morning glories decorating a perfect morning ride.

Our destination for the day was Ticul. See Chapter 9, Ticul: The Pearl of the South.

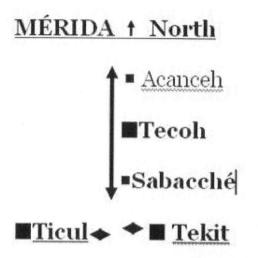

Tecoh to Cuzamá via Chiquilá, Sabacché, Ochil, and Chunkanán

Quiet country roads through scenic Yucatán are well worth the effort. Escaping Mérida's pushy-shovey horn honking, tail-gating belligerent bumper-to-bumper neurotic drivers is like flushing the proverbial toilet. It feels so good when it is finally gone.

Our escape Mérida bicycle trip is only a little over 30 kilometers long from Tecoh to Cuzamá but the narrow little road coupled with a brand new paved section connecting Ochil to Chunkanán makes a neat cycling loop with plenty of one of a kind photo opportunities.

We began this trip by bicycling seven kilometers from our home in Mérida to the Noreste bus terminal on Calle 67 and 50 in the city center.

An hour later we arrived in Tecoh with our little folding bicycles ready for the fresh air and tranquility that awaited us.

This is Tecoh where a few months of absence have seen many changes. The quiet streets once filled with silent bicycles and tricycle taxis are becoming noisier with the introduction of motorized tricycle taxis.

A change of government required a new paint job of all things municipal. So, it was out with the old and in with the new. Above is the city hall complex that last year was neatly painted in a distinctive buff color. Now it is politically correct with a color change to green.

After again shopping at Tecoh's colorful municipal market for some fruit and snacks, we headed out on the road to Sabacché, following the route of our previous trip.

After passing through Sabacché, we made our turn to the north, (left) onto the new road not yet on our map. For this insider piece of useful bicycling information we must thank www.bikemexico.com who offers superb Yucatán bicycle tours.

Our first stop was to see Cenote Chonkila, which is very close to this new road, but most of the area *cenotes* require a long trek through woods by meandering foot path.

Hanging from within the cave entrance on the north side of this *cenote* were some huge very active bee hives vigorously in operation. Swarms of busy bees find this location a nearly perfect environment, protected from the weather and predators with a ready supply of water at hand.

The aromatic scent of sweet honey was magnificently pervasive around the *cenote* where multitudes of bees became aggressive. They sent Jane wheeling on her bicycle down the road swatting the busy little critters away while frantically speeding into a strong headwind. She only received one sting because she was able to get them off her face while she hastily escaped.

This is one of over one hundred *cenotes* in this area designated on the map as *Zona de Cenotes*.

Most of these cenotes are situated in deep depressions in the rock with steep abrupt sides and no guard rails or warning signs. Be very careful because the fall into unknown depths of water is only half of your problem—rescue could possibly be a very long time in coming.

These *cenotes* can be spotted by the experienced person from a great distance because around them are found tall trees watered by their long roots reaching down into the *cenotes*.

The *cenotes* made it possible for the ancient Mayan people to prosper and thrive in this otherwise waterless arid place devoid of rivers and springs.

After a visit to Cenote Chonkila and a wild flight from the bees, we proceeded on to Chunkanán.

Chunkanán

Chunkanán is a very special little town because this is one of the last places in Yucatán still using the old Decauville narrow gauge railroad track, a remnant of the henequen era. By the late 1800s more than 4,500 kilometers of this half meter or 19 ½ inch wide track had been laid across the Yucatán. Horses were used to draw carriages on the track, thus transporting the product of the henequen plantations.

Here is the narrow gauge railroad leading into Chunkanán with its well worn tow path alongside. This century old rail system is actively in use today.

Jane is pictured with her Dahon twenty inch wheel folding bicycle that gives some perspective to the small size of the Decauville narrow gauge railroad track.

These tracks branch out to various *cenotes* meandering past old haciendas and active henequen fields. This area is much the same as it was in the heyday of that industry that made Yucatán the richest state in Mexico around the time of the two world wars of the 20th century.

The old hacienda town of Chunkanán is finding a rebirth in its economy attracting busloads of tourists all the way from the port city of Progreso. Cruise ship patrons come to ride the antique rail system.

Jane and I first visited Chunkanán in the early 1980s with friends, arriving by a narrow dirt road before tourism had become an industry. What made this trip memorable, besides our visit to a *cenote* with a deadly dangerous crumbling staircase, was our race with a six and a half foot long rattlesnake. At the same time as we rattled along riding in a cart on the Decauville tracks at a fast horse trot, the huge fat snake confined by a stone wall parallel to the track was actually slithering over the rough terrain faster than we were traveling.

From his office on the street, the boss or *jefe* of the Chunkanán rail service, Sr. Bolas, busily dispatches the one car horse drawn carriages on tours ranging from half hour up to three hour long guided trips. Visiting customers arrive by tricycle taxi from Cuzamá, a distance of four kilometers on a very quiet little paved road.

Like a page out of the last century, little Chunkanán reflects images of a time in Yucatán history when hacienda life was a prospering enterprise.

This is a small glimpse back into the unhurried past, before the days of a motorized world when the horse set the pace for travel.

Cuzamá has little to offer in the way of shopping or dining but does have historical significance and connects with cross-country buses and *colectivo* taxis to Mérida.

Getting there:
Noreste Bus Terminal – Mérida
Calle 67 between Calle 50 and 52
The Lus bus line has frequent departures.

Hotel Accommodations:
Posada Can Sacbe
Tekit

Chapter 9

Ticul

The Pearl of the South

Because of the many nearby attractions, it is good to home base in Ticul for several days. Bring your camera!

Take a city tour in a people powered tricycle taxi. Ticul is famous for its clay pottery and artistically ornamented reproductions of Mayan sculpture. You will be dazzled by what the town has to offer. Shoe manufacturing is a large scale cottage industry with numerous retail and wholesale outlets. Visit the 16th century recently restored Franciscan church, eat your way through the bustling municipal market, and take side trips to nearby points of interest.

The Puuc hills are nearby as are numerous Mayan ruins including Uxmal. Muna, the market town of Oxkutzcab, and Maní are easily reached by bike or bus.

Accommodations abound. Eating experiences range from excellent pizza to Mayan traditional dishes and *cocina económicas*. Bus and taxi service is as good as it gets.

This is bicycle country at its best. Try the route north through Sacalum with its 1500s fortress church perched upon an abnormal rock projection. From Sacalum you have options; east over a sacbe Mayan road to Xcanchakan or north to Abalá through the citrus groves, and then bus or taxi back to Mérida.

We first came to Ticul by narrow gauge train in the early 1980's and little did we know at that time that this relic of the past narrow gauge train, one of the last remaining in the world, was soon to vanish. What caught our eye at the time were the pottery works and myriad of ladies shoe shops where the shoes were made and sold.

On our many return trips over the years we have gradually discovered the numerous fascinating treasures that Ticul and its friendly people have to offer.

Ticul, 82 kilometers south of Mérida or about 50 miles, is known as the pearl of the south. Besides a number of strange and interesting things in the city, Ticul also has its unique geographical position adjacent to many remarkable monuments of the past.

We love the place. When it is the season of fresh corn, all of the delightfully delicious local foods made from it are only available in towns like Ticul where the *milpa* farmers bring their just harvested *maiz* (corn) to market.

When we arrive in Ticul, we usually head directly to the main market for *panuchos*. This alone makes the trip worthwhile. Still in the market, we devour freshly made *pool kan-es,* these elegant little deep fried cakes of *masa* (corn dough) are filled with *ibes,* a white lima bean. Topped with tangy sauce and diced sweet onion, they are scrumptious. Taste tempting treats abound.

Ticul's plaza is popular especially under the shade of the almond trees.

Afternoons when the shadows grow long, the plaza fills with vendors selling homemade eats and drinks. Little businesses are packed onto tricycles and feature snow cones and lots of snacks.

Fresh corn on the cob.

Fresh from the *milpa,* sweet hot corn on the cob is served with chili, salt, and lime juice. Jane and I cannot resist. This lady's business is portable and fits in the pail she carries to the plaza. Her wonderful product is in big demand and was sold out in just a few minutes. There is not enough room here to tell of all the delicious seasonal fresh corn delights available in these outlying towns.

More eats arrive; one lady has bags of peeled sweet oranges, mandarins, and fried corn snacks, which the customers love to sprinkle with hot sauce.

Evenings in the plaza are tranquil and pleasant for families and lovers.

The streets of Ticul are adorned with statuary depicting Mayan ritual ceremonies.

A street in Ticul.

Dance rehearsal in the plaza band-shell tells a lot about the pride of this very clean and prosperous city.

Ticul arch by Rómulo Rozo.

Perched atop a prominent hill overlooking Ticul is a distinctive arch that was constructed by the internationally famous sculptor Rómulo Rozo (1899-1964) back in the 1950's. The president of Mexico even arrived for the dedication.

The distinctive pink stone of this arch, and the *Monumento de la Patria* on the prestigious Paseo de Montejo in Mérida, came from a quarry on an adjacent hilltop on the road south to Santa Elena.

The Ticul arch is plagiarized in wall advertisements.

Rómulo Rozo left his distinctive creations all across Mexico.

One of Rómulo Rozo's most widely plagiarized works of art is this little figure known here as "Pedro". This is a copy of the sculptor's original piece *El Pensamiento*.

When *El Pensamiento* (The Thinker) was on exhibition at the library of Mexico City somebody placed a bottle of tequila in front of it, took a photo, and it was widely circulated around the world as the sleeping drunken Mexican—an image still thought of in the same way today.

The variety of paint jobs and size of "Pedro" seem endless—all the shops in Ticul sell them.

Ticul's proximity to the Puuc hill region and its numerous Mayan sites, plus good restaurants and hotels makes it an excellent location to use as headquarters for exploration of the area.

Getting there from Mérida
TAME Bus Terminal – Mérida
Mayab bus
Calle 69, between Calle 68 and 70

Colectivo Taxi to Santa Elena
Calle 30 between Calle 25a and Calle 25
6 a.m. to 8 p.m.

Hotel Accommodations:
Hotel Plaza Yucatán
Calle 23 #202 x 26 y 26a
97860 Ticul, Yucatán.
Tel: (997) 972-0484 Website: www.hotelplazayucatan.com

Ticul has many more accommodations, ranging from hotels to bungalows.

Related Chapters:
Chapter 14, Puuc Hill Region

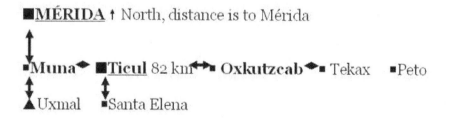

Chapter 10

Hunucmá

On the Road to Sisal

In February of every year, the Virgin of Tetiz makes its annual pilgrimage from the nearby town of Tetiz to the church at Hunucmá. The Virgin of Tetiz is escorted by a group of several thousand for its pilgrimage from Tetiz. The Virgin of Tetiz is then paraded daily for two weeks to visit different neighborhoods, and led by festively dressed citizens bedecked in their traditional costumes. At this time a two week fair is held in honor of the Virgin of Tetiz with folkloric dances, bull fights, concerts, plus expositions of handcrafts by Hunucmá artists. Local shoe manufacturers display their products; typical clothes and traditional foods are sold.

On the streets of clean and easy going Hunucmá, the Mayan traditional parade mixes the religious ceremonies of Catholicism with classic indigenous tradition that has persisted here in Yucatán for countless years, and extends back into antiquity.

Hunucmá, in Yucatec Maya means *agua de ciénega* or water of the lagoon.

Church of San Francisco, Hunucmá.

The original Hunucmá church was built in the 1500s. The structure you see today was constructed about 1700, and is of stacked stone construction. The building consumed the materials of a Mayan pyramid nearby.

Hunucmá is a 16th century Spanish mission town 23 km west of Mérida on an ancient *sacbe* road leading to the old port city of Sisal. The town was the area fruit provider until a recent hurricane destroyed many of the towering trees. From north of town to the Gulf of Mexico lie low flat lands subject to flooding from tropical disturbances and winter storms.

One of the streets of Hunucmá.

Hunucmá is a crossroads town and not an end destination, but that is one of the many charms that keep it out of the hurried push of the big city.

Hunucmá still has its colorful active street market. Shopping here has changed little over the centuries where locally produced meats and garden produce are found fresh daily.

Friendly faces on happy people are reminiscent of Yucatán in years gone by and a simpler life.

We spent some time in the clean main plaza of the town. We were surprised by the number of people who came to us and wanted to talk. Some wanted to practice their English, but others were just curious as to why we were in Hunucmá, and where we came from. Many were eager to share their stories of life in Hunucmá.

One young man we met in the plaza was 23 year old Luis Antonio Fritz Romero. He wanted to practice his English. Luis was employed at a local chicken processing plant. As a benefit of his employment, he had qualified for government help in buying a home. Private home ownership has been one of the better goals of the Mexican government.

Luis offered to show us some of the sites of Hunucmá, and also to take us to his new home. We biked with Luis to see his modest small house in a new subdivision of Hunucmá.

Luis and Jane in front of his new home.
Another interesting man we met in the plaza was Sr.
Soberanis, a retired journalist with the local newspaper.

**Sr. Soberanis holding a newspaper with an article that he
wrote for *El Diaro de Yucatán* in April of 2004 recalling
Fidel Castro's role in Yucatán in 1955.**

If you are up for some interesting adventure and a photo opportunity, consider a climb up the inside spiral staircase to the Hunucmá church roof.

From atop the Hunucmá church with its recently rebuilt roof, the jungle view looking east in the direction of Mérida reveals the colonial buildings surrounding the church. They were all built of materials salvaged from ancient Mayan temples that once stood here before the conquest nearly five hundred years ago.

The church front looking west from behind the belfry reveals the massive thickness of this *mamposteria*, stacked stone construction, that has survived the centuries.

Looking north from the church top you will see far off on the distant horizon a thin slice of blue that is the Gulf of Mexico in the direction of the port of Sisal.

This is the land of the Maya where their language is still spoken and understood. We had a filling, savory and satisfying midday meal in a *cocina económica* with its Mayan sign that says; "*Onene'ex way yano'one yam ja'na*" or "This is the place. Come on in and eat."

The price was right and the quantity and quality won't be beaten elsewhere. We ate the local specialty known as *poc chuc*, which is thinly sliced pork grilled along with onion and served with tortillas, rice, and a thin black bean soup. Freshly made hot sauces usually need to be tested before spooning on because some are blisteringly hot.

On a narrow paved side road south of Hunucmá is the quiet hacienda town of San Antonio Chel where activity appeared to be in some sort of suspended animation.

The ancient and neglected main entry gate to San Antonio Chel.

Hacienda San Antonio Chel was actively part of the henequen industry until nearly twenty years ago when the business nearly collapsed.

One of several of the humble little abodes of San Antonio Chel was bedecked with a hand painted Virgin of Guadalupe, which is uniquely Mexican.

We visited the ruins of Sihunchen on the road from Hunucmá to San Antonio Chel.

Trail on the outer perimeter of the ruins of Sihunchen.

If you happen to hike the trail around to the outer perimeter of Sihunchen, the lovely jungle path abounding in unspoiled native vegetation and innumerable birds will make all your efforts worthwhile. The heavily looted remains of these Mayan temples are now only marked by scattered detritus. Twenty years ago these woods did not exist because the area was fully cultivated in henequen. Some henequen plants can still be seen in places hanging on in the woods.

After over four hundred years of being quarried for building materials, heaps of rock rubble is all that remain of the Mayan temples of Sihunchen. At the time of the ancient Maya, Sihunchen had a celestial observatory similar to the one at Chichén Itzá. Known locally as *los cerros* or the hills, the rock refuse that is still on this site is astonishingly huge. It has to be seen in order to grasp the vastness of these remains. Consider this, all this rock had to be carried here on the backs of the ancient Maya without the aid of any machinery.

Biking, bird watching and photo-ops abound in this area around Hunucmá. It is so close to Mérida but so far removed in its isolated tranquility. The area is prolific with seldom traveled roads and innumerable classic haciendas haunted by history that awaits your visit. Don't spoil the ambiance—bike it!

Sisal

Twenty-three kilometers from Hunucmá is the fishing village of Sisal with beautiful white sand beaches. During the henequen boom in Yucatán, Sisal was the principal port for Mérida and Yucatán. Sisal lent its name to the fiber (sisal) that was shipped from its port. The port of Sisal was founded in 1811 and has a fortress and an old lighthouse. After the development of Progreso (see Chapter 11, El Puerto de Progreso), shipping was diverted when Progreso became the official port of Yucatán.

Sisal is worth a visit if for no other reason than to eat some of the best seafood in Yucatán at Restaurante Muelle de Sisal, located directly on the beach. Sisal is a small place and the restaurant is easy to find.

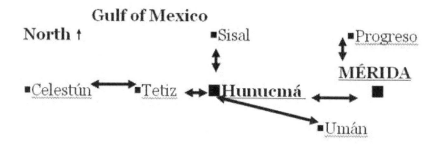

Getting there:
Noreste Bus Terminal – Mérida
Calle 67 between Calle 50 and 52
Oriente has frequent buses to Hunucmá.

Hotel Accommodations:
There are several small hotels in Sisal.

Chapter 11

El Puerto de Progreso
A popular beach town with white sand beaches, sunshine, fresh air, and delicious seafood.

Progreso is Mérida's seaport and a cruise ship destination located on Yucatán's north coast. Five hundred miles of tropical coke bottle green Gulf of México waters stretch out in all directions. Fresh briny sea breezes make this relatively new town in old Mexico positively pleasant. Europeans and Canadians make Progreso their wintertime home.

The Gulf of Mexico beach at Progreso.

These Mexican waters have been a link to the outside world from ancient times. Before the Spanish conquistadors arrived, the Chantal Maya of Tabasco, with their huge sailing sea-going cargo canoes, came to collect sun dried sea salt from the extensive lagoons that rim the Yucatán peninsula.

A British Admiralty chart of Yucatán from 1840 only listed "Huts" in the spot where Progreso is today. In 1840 it was only accessible by boat.

Today Progreso is a world port with a population of nearly 54,000 and Yucatán's conduit for commerce. Commercial fishing, cruise ship tourism, and a large retirement community have built a solid economic base.

A trip from Mérida to Progreso is easy. The secret to this easy trip is that we take the Autoprogreso bus that departs its terminal located on Calle 62 between Calle 65 and 67 in downtown Mérida. It can also be flagged down along its route.

We stow our folding bicycles in the bus luggage space for the forty-five minute ride in air-conditioned comfort. Buses depart every 10 to 20 minutes, and we often wave them down near our home.

Jane seated at the Progreso seashore.

The above photo contains several interesting items. On the right is the long pier extending 6.5 kilometers out into the Gulf of México that links Yucatán to the entire world of maritime commerce with container and bulk freight. Cruise ships also call at this pier several times a week bringing thousands of tourists with each visit.

The first 1.75 kilometer long portion of the pier was completed in 1941, and it is now the oldest surviving reinforced concrete structure submerged in sea water in the world.

Also in this photo is an amazing contrast. Straight out from shore, there are a number of protruding pilings, some covered with birds. This is what remained in 2011 from a concrete commercial fishing pier built in 1960 using steel reinforcement rods. The old 1941 pier continues on to this day. It was built with stainless steel rod, unscathed by time, and it takes a heavier pounding than the original builders had ever imagined. In 2012 the commercial fishing pier was rebuilt using standard steel reinforcement...its days are already numbered.

When cruise ships arrive, the streets of Progreso fill with visitors, many of whom have never set foot in a foreign country. Not speaking Spanish many opt for a guided city bus tour ...a good orientation option.

On days when cruise ships are in port, swarms of street vendors hawk interesting artistic memorabilia and two craft markets are set up.

The paradox of Progreso is the vast difference in living standards that seem to be separated by more than a century. A common sight on the streets are these little horse carts that deliver everything including ice. Bring your camera.

Traffic congestion has yet to arrive in Progreso, and here Jane and I stop to check out one of the many tributes to social conscience; a bust of martyred governor Felipe Carrillo Puerto. Governor Carrillo Puerto has a fascinating story behind him.

After México's nearly three hundred years of slavery, the Mexican-American War, the Yucatán's fight for sovereignty, the protracted Caste War that began in 1847, and next the turbulent revolutionary war that laid the ground for social reform, Felipe Carrillo Puerto became governor of Yucatán with a platform of workers' rights, land reform, and equality for the indigenous Mayan people. Elected in 1922, Felipe was assassinated. Opposition factions put him and all his brothers before a firing squad in January, 1924.

With the momentum that Felipe Carrillo Puerto's efforts generated, two schools were constructed in Progreso by labor unions: *Maniobras Maritima* by the dock workers' union, and *Martires de Chicago*, funded and constructed by the henequen workers' union. The school was named in honor of the Martyrs of Chicago. The anarchists accused of a bombing at a labor union rally in Haymarket Square in Chicago, Illinois, in 1886 were called the Martyrs of Chicago. The Haymarket affair inspired the modern celebration of May Day. These schools are still in operation and now have government support.

A Glance at Progreso in 1946

Journalist Lilo Linke visited Progreso in 1946 and left an interesting account of her visit in her book *Magic Yucatan.*

> *El Progreso* lies only twenty-four miles north of Mérida, connected by a smooth highway. Chicle, the raw material of chewing-gum, and henequen are exported from there.
>
> The workers of the port are organized in unions which resemble castes... And always there is a lot of jealousy between them.
>
> But those men have one thing in common: ambition for the future of their children...We went first to that of the "Martyrs of Chicago", the Association of Henequen Workers, who deal with the henequen until it reaches the docks. Their school was poor. Each hard-used piece of furniture wore a pathetic look...
>
> It was in this same school that I heard for the first time of Felipe Carrillo Puerto, Yucatan's Socialist leader, who was shot in 1924. I had heard German children pronounce the name of Hitler— metallic, triumphant, a dagger raised into the air. But the people of Yucatán, even these fourteen-year-olds, grew quiet as the name of their hero rolled softly off their tongues...

Downtown Progreso

On the west side of the city center park is the elegant and stately municipal building that reflects the sudden surge of henequen revenue that flowed through this little port town.

Inside the stately municipal building, pink marble stairs and elegant cast statuary are but some of the many adornments that port commerce has generated.

The mezzanine balcony contains an interesting collection of oil paintings by Favila depicting port related historical events like the arrival of Mexican President Porfirio Diaz in 1906. Another painting depicts the founding of the *El Puerto de Progreso de Castro* when Juan Miguel Castro Martin, the mayor, dedicated it in the 1870's. It is well worth your effort to see this superb collection of oil paintings depicting history as it happened. This collection is one of Progreso's treasures.

Progreso municipal building, a short walk up calle 80 from the bus terminal. This is the same street as the lighthouse (*faro*) and municipal market. The street goes to the waterfront.

For a look at more scenes of Progreso from years ago, visit the restaurant El Cordobés located across the street and to the north of the city center park (corner of Calle 80 and Calle 31). There you will find paintings by Mario Trejo that tell much of the story of the old Progreso: small open sailing boats catching the afternoon onshore breeze to bring the fishermen home, henequen bales carted out to be shipped to distant destinations, Diamond Rio buses, and the little horse drawn rail carts shuffling passengers and freight up and down the pier.

We enjoy coffee and reminiscing in El Cordobés, a place that has changed little from the time of our first visit in the early 1980s, but when we want to eat, we go to one of our two favorite restaurants in Progreso: Sol y Mar or Yum Ixpu.

Sol y Mar Restaurant
Calle 78 on the corner with Calle 25, downtown.

When Jane's cousin and his wife Phyllis from Texas arrived in Progreso on a Carnival cruise ship we met them on Calle 80 in front of the lighthouse. Our first stop was for coffee at Sol y Mar...and we stayed for lunch.

Phyllis is a *fajita aficionado* and asked about the beef fajitas. We told her that a friend raved about the chicken *fajitas.*

My comment: "If you have been in Mexico so long that the beef starts to taste good, you have been in Mexico too long."

Phyllis persisted and ordered the beef fajitas. The order

arrived and Phyllis ate with relish. She not only raved about the fajitas, but she exclaimed that they were the best she had ever had...and she is from Texas, home to the world's best fajitas.

Karl had the house special and rated it excellent. What more could we ask for: our fish filets were delicious and our guests were happy.

Phyllis enjoying *fajitas.*

Give Sol y Mar a try. They open for breakfast at 8:30 a.m.

Yum Ixpu
Calle 31, between Calle 94 and Calle 96.

Yum Ixpu is where the locals go for seafood fresh from the fishermen.

To get to Yum Ixpu from Progreso's main plaza, go west on Calle 31. Cross Calle 94 and look for Yum Ixpu upstairs on the north side. Open from 11 a.m. to 6 p. m. Closed Monday.

Yum Ixpu: Good seafood, cold beer, and friendly service.

Every day in Mexico is an adventure just waiting for you to discover.

Along the coast east of Progreso are the beach towns of Chicxulub Puerto, Telchac Puerto, San Crisanto, Chabihau, and Dzilám de Bravo. A short bicycle ride east from the city center, the beaches become quiet and inviting.

The little village of Chicxulub Puerto, most noted for the fact that this is the epicenter of the meteorite that struck 65 million years ago with such an impact that it disrupted life on earth and caused the end of the dinosaur era, has a small market, pharmacy, hardware store, and several tortilla shops. One thing that they have several of are *cantinas* that specialize in beer and *botanas* (snacks) plus a local specialty of deep fried fish.

Chicxulub Puerto is a quiet out of the way spot until July and August when the summer crowd overwhelms it. In the dead of winter and with no snow, Chicxulub Puerto attracts many visitors, especially Canadians.

Information for Cruise Ship Passengers
Getting from Progreso to Mérida

The bus terminal in Progreso is located between Calle 80 and 82 and between Calle 27 and 29. The terminal has three street entrances. The north entrance is just south of the light house which can easily be seen from the entrance on Calle 27. If you arrive here by bus you will enter from calle 82, the same street that comes directly from the cruise ship pier. On cruise ship days, the entrance on Calle 29 is through a craft market. The third entrance is from Calle 82.

Cruise ship arrivals have several options here.

Autoprogreso has representatives in the terminal pitching their guided bus tours to Mérida and a number of Mayan ruins. Another option is to make your own self-guided tour to Mérida. Buy a round trip ticket (*ida y vuelta*). Buses depart for Merida every 10 or 15 minutes.

Website: www.autoprogreso.com/

Mérida to Progreso

The Autoprogreso bus terminal in Mérida is located on Calle 62, between Calles 65 and 67 in downtown Mérida. Merida's center and downtown plaza is located just a block and a half north of the Autoprogreso terminal. See chapter 19 for more Mérida bus information.

Another option is a taxi, if the price is acceptable it is a chance to converse with a Mexican and get his recommendations. The taxi can deliver you and your group all the way back out to your ship.

You don't have to be a cruise ship passenger to take the tours offered by Autoprogreso. The catch is that they are only offered on the days that cruise ships are in port. For more information visit their website.

Come to Progreso for the fun, the sun, and the seafood.

Chapter 12

Yaxhachen – Oxkutzcab to Tekax

Kiuic and Our Puuc Hills Jungle Experience

Our jungle escape would take us on an overnight excursion into the remote Puuc hills and the Mayan temple ruins of Kiuic. What makes this place so very interesting and unusual is the fact that it is not open to the general public. Check it out at: www.kiuic.org.

Kiuic was first visited, sketched and described by the world famous traveler and author John L. Stephens who published in 1843, *Incidents of Travel in Yucatan*. In the book he describes the place he called *Kewick*. In this book there is a sketch of a *palapa* home he called *casa real* where he and his traveling group stayed. Though Stephens describes the *casa real* as being filled with fleas and the walls of mud, he had this to say;

"We had seldom experienced higher satisfaction on reaching a new and unknown field of ruins, though perhaps this was owing somewhat to the circumstances of finding ourselves, after a hot and perplexing ride, safely arrived at our place of destination."

Located in the southern tip of the state of Yucatán, Kiuic's wilderness is hauntingly beautiful, especially with the multitude of Mayan temples that speak of one of the greatest civilizations that this world has ever known. The heritage of this incredible civilization is still actively found here in the area's place names, cuisine, language, farming techniques, and even their thatched roof *palapas* houses that are much like those of their ancestors.

We began our jungle experience when Jane and I bicycled to the TAME bus terminal in downtown Mérida. A friend joined us for the bus trip to Oxkutzcab, 100 km south.

Our two-hour scenic bus tour took us through all of the off the main road towns and villages along the way to our destination of Oxkutzcab. Jane and I disembarked with our bicycles. We arranged a tricycle taxi for our traveling companion.

Jane and I set out across town to check on a hotel that had been recommended to us. The Hotel Puuc was acceptable but the location left something to be desired for our plans. We opted for the Hotel Trujeque located on the city central plaza, a place where we had stayed previously.

Would you believe that when Jane and I turned into the hotel parking area, we somehow had lost our traveling companion and the tricycle taxi driver too? We checked into the hotel and still no sign of our nomadic companion and her taxi driver. Had he absconded with her?

I set out by bicycle in search but I found no sign of them. I decided to return to the hotel and wait. On the way back to the hotel they pulled along side me like nothing had happened. We later learned that our nomadic friend was having a difficult time explaining to the taxi driver in her broken Spanish that she wanted him to follow us.

The taxi driver pictured with our friend on the streets of Oxkutzcab.

That afternoon after a fabulously generous and delicious meal at a local *cocina económica*, we all struck off to find our own adventures. Our friend rented a taxi like the one above and visited several local homes, picked fruit, and visited the hermitage of the Virgin of Pilar that sits high atop a hill overlooking the city.

Jane and I struck off near sunset on our bicycles to follow some wild jungle trails that passed aged haciendas, and we were treated to a cacophony of tropical birds chirping. This was our kind of paradise.

On the streets of Oxkutzcab we watched a man hand chiseling this stone used to grind corn in a local corn mill where tortillas are made. He told us that the process needed to be repeated every three months, and it took him two hours using only his trained eye and his simple little hammer. His business was doing all of the area mills.

This full-mooned night we shared our afternoon adventure stories while we ate *salbutes* and *panuchos* in the main market. They were not only savory but also very affordable. After eating we walked the streets. We found a liquor store where we drank a beer. The wary owner cautioned us that we were to conceal our beer if the police arrived because he didn't have a license.

Thus, day one of our jungle adventure tour ended.

Day two: After a good snooze, we revisited the main market for shopping and photos. We met our friend coming

120

out of the old church. She had visited the big downtown church and managed to get locked in—and our second day of adventures was just beginning!

This is the courtyard of the old Oxkutzcab church where our friend was mistakenly locked in. The church and surrounding buildings have recently been magnificently restored.

Our bus to our next destination, high up in the Puuc hills at the Mayan village of Yaxhachen, was waiting across the street from our hotel. My wife and I loaded our bicycles aboard the second class bus because it had the most room inside. Our nomadic cohort opted for the first class bus and paid fifteen pesos.

Buses to Yaxhachen; second class on the right and first class left.

At 11:30 a.m. we rolled away for another adventure. The entertainment aboard our rickety old bus was so intense we became inundated with the nonstop routine of the two men in the following photo.

Entertainment aboard the Yaxhachen bus; *loco y lococido* (crazy and crazier). The man on the left is Omar Antonio Bacalar, an herb and natural medicine man.

These once a day buses would carry us up the incredibly steep hills and then an hour later deliver us to the small Mayan village of Yaxhachen at the end of the road where we would spend the night in the Mayan home of Adalio and Paula.

Our lodging place in the Mayan village of Yaxhachen.

We slept in our hammocks in their living room and ate the local traditional food prepared over an open fire. Hand made tortillas using freshly ground local corn left a lasting impression and a yearning to return for that special treat. These are experiences enjoyed by very few visitors.

That afternoon after *puchero*, a Mayan meat and vegetable stew, and an interesting conversation with Paula, our hostess, we were treated to a countryside *milpa* bike tour guided by Adalio, Paula's husband.

This trip alone was more than worth the effort of our entire trip. Totally devoid of all motor noises, we silently glided along on bicycles through the Puuc hills and ancient Mayan *milpas* unchanged for thousands of years. We had now gone past the end of the road, and we were just following a footpath that has been used by the locals for countless generations. We rode until dusk in this pristine dream world to the neighboring state border of Campeche. It was a rare exploration not to be duplicated.

Adalio is in front of his home ready to roll with his bicycle, machete, and shot gun.

Adalio took us to see his bee hives and then asked how much longer we wanted to ride. We were concerned about the fading sunlight so our friend asked Adalio what time it was. Adalio gazed at the horizon and replied 5 o'clock. She had her doubts about his accuracy so she pulled out her McDonalds watch to check the time. Adalio was right!

After copious quantities of tacos for dinner prepared by Paula, we took a full moon light stroll through the gently quiet village of Yaxhachen, devoid of traffic and blissfully quiet—yes, a slice of paradise!

This very cool clear moonlit February night promised to be especially memorable. We would sleep in our own hammocks hung within an authentic Mayan home, guests of real Mayans. From our many years of experience in this part of the world, we knew the further from the sea the cooler the night, plus these typical thatched Mayan *palapas* are excellent natural air circulators automatically pulling warm air up and out. We bundled up and slept quietly and very cozy.

Day three: After a good sleep, we packed up while Paula was busy tending her cooking fire and preparing another huge stack of hand patted fresh tortillas for our breakfast. After Paula managed to stuff us to capacity with her savory tacos, Jane and I departed on our bicycles. We glided silently through town blessed with sweet fresh air, solitude, and the long shadows of an early tropical morning. Then we rode six kilometers to the Kiuic reserve through wild forest to rendezvous with our tour group arriving by car.

The director of Kiuic, James Callaghan, along with his wife Ruby, made our visit and tour into a fun, educational and rewarding experience. We immediately felt warm and friendly vibes from them both while we were cordially invited to rest in the shady jungle ambiance of the newly constructed dining hall. Copious quantities of fresh squeezed orange juice and tropical fruit were offered as welcoming hospitality.

Next, James gave an orientation speech followed by a very interesting walking tour.

Our tour took us to the remains of the *casa real* where the famous explorer and author John L. Stephens and his crew stayed on their journey through the Yucatán back in 1840. One of the roof support timbers was still standing, and there still remained some plaster on the wall behind it.

James Callaghan gave his inspiring and informative presentation to our tour group. He explained that the name Kaxil Kiuic means in Maya, the forest market or plaza.

Ruby was the coordinator of just about everything that takes place at Kiuic including hospitality and meals. She makes it all happen.

After the tour, it was back to the dining hall for Mayan style *puchero*, accompanied with lots of freshly hand made real corn tortillas. Then a few minutes to unpack, shower and a 5 minute rest in our newly built two room cabins before rallying for our 3 p.m. Mayan ruins and nature hike. The hiking tour lasted until the sun slipped away at the end of the day.

Though we visited numerous Mayan ruins at Kiuic, we only were able to see a small fraction of the ones there. The woods are literally full of them.

In the evening we were treated to "all you could eat" Yucatecan style tamales. Our time was spent getting acquainted, sharing thoughts, and interesting stories, which prepared us for a wonderfully quiet and peaceful snooze. We slipped off to sleep with our minds dancing full of visions from a magnificent and memorable day.

Day four: We arose with the sun, packed our gear, ate a hardy breakfast, and silently pedaled away on our bicycles. The rest of the group took a half-day guided hiking tour with James Callaghan.

Jane and I had 50 kilometers of hills and a strong head wind this day so an early start was imperative.

We had dreamed for many years of some day bicycling all the way across the Puuc hills. Puuc in Mayan means the edge of the hills or where the hills begin. This bike trip proved to be one of the best of our 40 plus years of cycling together.

Cycling across the Puuc hills leaving the small town of Xul where we made our first rest stop. Here the rolling terrain is filled with interesting surprises that include old Spanish haciendas and quaint chapels interspersed with Mayan ruins.

The explorer and author John L. Stephens visited this village of Xul in 1840 and gave an exquisite and interesting account of that encounter in his 1843 book, *Incidents of Travel in Yucatan.* I won't spoil your good read here. Read the book and discover for yourself this interesting link in cultural evolution.

Our next rest stop was at Xohuayan, a Mayan village perched high atop a steep hill that we huffed and puffed to climb. The climb warranted a rest stop.

At the small village of Xohuayan, we stopped in front of a store to take a break and cool in the shade.

We were about to eat a light snack of fresh tortillas with salt and a glass of water when an inquisitive crowd gathered.

Only one man spoke Spanish, the others only Mayan including the children. The Spanish speaking man saw us eating only tortillas and told us he didn't have much food in his house, only a pot of beans, but we were welcome to share it with him.

We graciously declined his offer because we have found eating too much on a long bicycle ride puts lead in our legs.

Children carrying freshly boiled corn from home to the *molino*, (mill) to be ground into *masa*, (dough to make tortillas).

Leaving town we sizzled downhill flying along and smoking our brakes as we went on our lovely way across the Puuc hills to Tekax.

Tekax is a Mayan town rich in Spanish heritage, which reflects its influence in the distinctive colonial buildings of the town.

There almost always seems to be some sort of festival going on in Tekax, and we have enjoyed many of them. The most popular is in honor of San Diego de Abalá held the first part of November every year. This is a weeklong affair with parades, fireworks, dances, bullfights, and a fair. It is not to be missed.

After a long day on our bikes, we weren't looking for a festival. We were happy that our hotel room at the Posada del Carmen in Tekax, adjacent to our friend Carlos Carrillo's restaurant El Huinic de al Ermita, was ready and waiting for us. Some of the members of our tour group from Kiuic were enjoying dinner when we arrived and asked us to join them.

They had arrived by car so they were cool and relaxed; we on the other hand were hot, sweaty, and spent. Our first priority was a cool shower followed by a peaceful nap. Then with our bodily batteries charged and our appetites honed, we went down to a two-hour dining extravaganza—heavenly! It was magnificent, as usual, and we had the same waiter we have had for the past 25 years when we used to arrive in Tekax by narrow gauge railroad train from Mérida.

A happy and contented Jane with our waiter, Genaro, at the Restaurant El Huinic de la Ermita: a place where we tend to linger an hour or two over dinner.

Getting there:
TAME Bus Terminal – Mérida
Calle 69, between Calle 68 and 70

Noreste Bus Terminal – Mérida
Calle 67, between Calle 50 and 52
Bus and *colectivo* taxi connections to Mérida are frequent.

Colectivo taxis depart from the area of Parque San Juan between Calle 62 and 64 and Calle 69a.

Related chapters:
Chapter 3, Oxkutzcab
Chapter 13, Tekax
Chapter 14, Puuc Hills Region

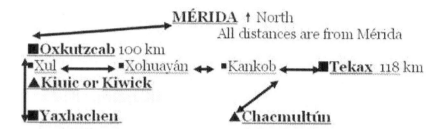

Chapter 13

Tekax

Friendly Faces of Tekax

Long time friends, Tekax mayor Carmen Navarrete, Carlos Carrillo Góngora, and John and Jane Grimsrud.

Tekax is a charming colonial Mayan town at the foot of the Puuc hills. It is in the process of renovation, thanks to Mayor Carmen Navarrete. Tourism is being featured and takes advantage of the area's natural assets.

Tekax is proud of the *Ruta de las Cavernas* (cave route) that attracts exploration by world travelers. Off-road bicycle routes abound and are continually being developed. Be sure to visit the new tourist office in the municipal building.

Tekax is a place we return to again and again to visit friends, the caves, bike the back country roads, and explore the Chacmultún ruins.

In Yucatec Maya, Tekax means place of the forest. Tekax de Alvaro Obregón is the seat of the municipality of Tekax.

Tekax is steeped in turbulent history from the early 17th century when the huge San Juan Bautista church was completed after suffering a disastrous construction collapse. The 200 foot long vaulted ceiling of the church gives a deceptive proportion to this massive structure that was used as a fortress during the Caste War when its priceless colonial *retablos* were destroyed.

The colonial town, at one time the largest city in Yucatán, has a number of appealing points of interest; the hermitage hilltop chapel, *la ermita de San Diego*, built in 1645, commands an inspiring panoramic view and is especially good at sunset. The plaza, with its great church, was described as the finest in Yucatán, and the market still has small town back country colonial time's charm. For many, the spectacular caves are the principal attraction to Tekax.

Take a tricycle taxi guided city tour and discover one of the finest examples of colonial era construction—the town is simply charming.

We have been visiting Tekax, one of our favorite colonial Yucatán towns, since the days of the old narrow gauge railway train nearly a quarter century ago, and we have been eating at the same restaurant all these years.

Carlos Carrillo Góngora, owner of El Huinic de la Ermita restaurant.

It is worth the trip to Tekax just for the traditional *poc-chuc* dish served at El Huinic de la Ermita. Thinly sliced pork marinated in the juice of the sour orange is grilled over charcoal and served with a variety of savory sauces. To make the meal most memorable, handmade tortillas are furnished in unlimited quantities.

The breakfast at El Huinic de la Ermita restaurant of *huevos a la Mexicana* is enough to sustain an active bicycler until noon, and is meant for a Mayan king. You may think that we only come to Tekax to eat. It is definitely one of the main attractions.

El Huinic de la Ermita restaurant is located at the foot of the 17th century *ermita* chapel, San Diego de Alcalá. The chapel is prominently and conspicuously perched above the city.

A very pleasant and especially romantic thing to do is to climb the stone stairs meandering up to the chapel in early evening to watch the city lights pop on as the stars above begin to fill the tropical twilight sky.

What is *El Huinic*?

El Huinic is a Mayan field worker who has tended the farmlands of Yucatán for countless centuries. A day's ration of water is carried in a gourd at his waist along with a bag containing his *pozol*. He will mix the *pozol* with water and some chili peppers for his day's sustenance. The traditional garb consists of a small brim hat, white shirt, trousers rolled up to his knees, simple flat sandals of *henequen* twine, cloth pouch and water gourd hung from his waist. His universal cutting tool shaped like a hook is called a *coá*.

The tallest structure in Tekax is three stories and is nearly two hundred years old. It is located on the street that leads to the hilltop chapel.

A description of that unusual building was made in 1840 by author John L. Stephens when he ventured into town on horseback after an extensive back country tour of exploring and sketching remote area Mayan ruins. He was the first to do so.

The city abounds in authentic colonial buildings. Bring your camera!

Side trips from Tekax are many. One of our favorites is to visit the Mayan archeology site of Chacmultún high up in the Puuc hills and serenely detached from civilization.

Kankab and Chacmultún

Colectivo **taxi to Kankab.**

Day two of one of our Tekax outings finds us, after breakfast, boarding the *colectivo* taxi at the city center park. Our bicycles are stowed on top of the van. We are headed up into the Puuc hills to the tiny town of Kankab. Kankab in Mayan means red earth.

We were on our way to bicycle to the remote Mayan ruins of Chacmultún from Kankab.

The taxi dropped us at the main plaza of Kankab, and we were almost immediately surrounded by children who were filing out of the school across the street. The first little boy spotted us and yelled; "Gringos"! Then he ran over to us with a group of his friends and came up to me and yelled; "War"!

After spending time with the town kids, we were on our way by bicycle up the hill to the Mayan ruins of Chacmultún. In Mayan this means red stone, and these unique ruins are made of red colored local rock.

Chacmultún

This beautiful ancient Mayan city built of red stone was continuously occupied from 300 B.C. until the time the Spaniards arrived in the 16th century. From A.D. 600 to 1000, Chacmultún was an important religious and political center.

Nearly five hundred years have passed from the time that the Spanish conquistadors arrived and plundered the Mayan people, and their ancient cities.

View from the ruins of Chacmultún.

We first visited Chacmultún in the early 1980's, and have witnessed in the passing years the rapid rate of degradation that has exponentially accelerated. Two recent major hurricanes toppled many of the temple stones. The temple mounds were invaded by gigantic tree roots, plus squatters building cooking fires inside the buildings have destroyed some of the ornate Mayan wall paintings. At least this place did not meet the fate of numerous other Mayan temples in Yucatán of just being used as a source of building materials for conquistador construction projects.

The view from the ruins of Chacmultún high up in the Puuc hills, where we had our lunch in total privacy, is lovely and spectacular. We were lucky enough to be the only visitors to the site on that day. Of all of the Mayan ruins we have ever visited over all the years, this is our very favorite.

From here it is nearly all downhill back to Tekax, a distance of ten kilometers—our kind of biking!

A metate of the red stone from Chacmultún.

Some years ago, a worker that helped build our home in Mérida, José Chí, gave us an ancient and well worn *metate* that his grandmother had given to him. That ancient *metate* was nearly ground through by countless years of heavy use. The *metate* is a carved stone used by the ancients to grind their corn. This *metate* is from the Tekax area and made of the unique rosy red stone found there. The little round cylinder shaped stone used on the *metate* is called a *mano*.

Getting there:
TAME Bus Terminal – Mérida
Calle 69 between Calle 68 and 70
Mayab bus

Colectivo vans leave from Parque San Juan
Calle 62 and Calle 69a
Bus and *colectivo* taxi connections to Mérida are frequent.

Restaurant
Restaurant El Huinic de La Ermita
Calle 61 #201 x Calle 50
Tekax, Yucatán   Open 8 a.m. to 9 p.m.

Las Cavernas (caves)
Sabac-ha, X'mait, Chocantes, Oxpe'jol y San Agustín
Contact Mario Novelo marionovelo25@hotmail.com
Also inquire for guides in the *turismo* tourist office in the
municipal building in Tekax.

Related chapters:
Chapter 12, Yaxhachen – Oxkutzcab to Tekax

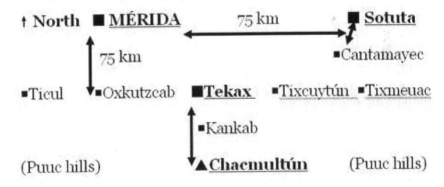

Chapter 14

Puuc Hill Region

A visit to Oxkutzcab, the Ruta Puuc, and Santa Elena

The Puuc hill region is an area of semiarid low tropical jungle set in rolling hills located about 80 kilometers south of Mérida.   In this remote area are dozens of Mayan ruins dating from between 300 B.C. and A.D. 1200. They are collectively known as *La Ruta Puuc* (The Puuc Route). The most famous of the ruins within the area is Uxmal.   In the time of the ancient Mayan cities, which are now in ruins, they were connected by raised roadways called *sacbe* (smooth, straight and nearly level white surfaced and plastered pedestrian roadways linking important Mayan sites).

A good home base for excursions into the Puuc can be found in Muna, Ticul, Santa Elena, Oxkutzcab, or Tekax. All are nearby and offer accommodations and points of interest.

We invite you to share another of our pleasurable bike-bus eco-friendly adventures into the Puuc region.

Beginning in Mérida, after our five kilometer bike ride to the Tikal Restaurant on Calle 57 downtown for their breakfast special, we boarded the 9:30 a.m. *Lus* bus at the Noreste terminal at Calle 67 and 50 bound for Oxkutzcab. This three hour Sunday morning bus trip is a perfect starter for a Yucatán back country sightseeing journey.

An additional bonus of the second class bus is the opportunity to interact with wandering troubadours serenading the passengers for tips, and with local vendors of exotic traditional Mayan handicrafts, foods, desserts, and beverages—something not experienced on first class direct buses.

We traveled the back roads of Yucatán, entered the small colonial villages, and got a first hand look at the colorful local population, many of whom would be our traveling companions.

Just twenty kilometers out of Mérida at Acanceh, we had already left behind the big city rush, and our back country exploration was just beginning.

Bustling open air markets, festive circus carnivals, wooden scaffold bullfight rings, jubilant marching processions, street vendors, people powered tricycles taxis, and more; all this created a cacophony of bizarre sounds commingled with the tantalizing olfactory enticement of regional cooking, which produced almost uncontrollable mouth watering temptations.

Our meandering bus route next took us to Tecoh, Telchaquillo, Tekit, Mamá, Chumayel, Teabo, Tipikal, Maní, and on to Oxkutzcab.

We are not strangers to these fascinating places.

Oxkutzcab

Oxkutzcab is the hub of many interesting adventures that are far too numerous for just one visit. They include the marketplace, restored colonial church, hill-top hermitage chapel, plus side trips to the Grutas Loltún. See Chapter 3, Oxkutzcab.

This story presents another side trip adventure possibility.

Day two of our journey begins before 7 a.m. when we roll out of the convenient Hotel Trujeque in Oxkutzcab across from the city center park with our fully provisioned Dahon folding bicycles bound for the local taxi stand adjacent to the tortilla shop on the west side of the main market.

There was no set or posted price for our destination to the Mayan ruins of Labná so haggling would be required. This can be a lot of fun if done in a good natured way. Six taxi drivers joined in the negotiation and price quotes began to fly around—100, 200, 150 pesos were mentioned, and I suggested 50. Oh no! The banter goes on and someone suggests 120 pesos. We nod yes, and we were on our way.

Jesús, our taxi driver, and Jane survey the packed and stacked cargo as we ready ourselves to depart Oxkutzcab.

One of our folding bicycles would go inside the taxi, and the other was lashed along with empty orange crates in the trunk. Jesús had come to town from a village in the Puuc with those orange crates full earlier in the morning.

Jesús had an interesting story to tell. He and his family had left the little fishing village of Champotón, Campeche, thirty years earlier when the fishing industry collapsed from over fishing and petrol chemical pollution. Jesús has a tradition of large families and was one of eighteen. He has thirteen children of his own. His mother died at the age of 102.

He must have had some pangs of conscience about the fare or actually got to like us because he pulled off onto a dirt road and picked us a bag of fresh oranges, which were a welcome supplement to our cross-country diet. By the way, the angelic aroma of orange blossoms in the Puuc hills this season makes you want to drink in the intoxicatingly sweet air and linger.

Our taxi dropped us off high up in the Puuc hills at Labná, where we had our breakfast in the peaceful jungle tranquility before the gate opened at 8 a.m. We traveled light on our excursion. For this day's travel we did however pack along eight liters of drinking water and 500 ml. of *Suero*, an electrolyte replacement drink of essential bodily salts necessary for hydration when heavily perspiring. All pharmacies stock this product and have it in flavored liquid form and also in envelopes of powder to mix with water.

Labná

Labná in the early morning is worth the effort. You can glimpse the ornate stone work of the ancient Maya and their style of arch building.

Jane framed by the famous corbelled arch of Labná.

Ecomuseo del Cacao

Located between the Mayan archeological sites of Labná and Xlapak is the new Ecomuseo del Cacao (museum of chocolate). The museum is located on the grounds of Tikul

Plantation. In a tour of the museum you will learn the fascinating history of chocolate in the Mayan culture, and you will be served a traditional Mayan drink prepared using chocolate. The museum is open to the public every day from 9 a.m. to 6 p.m. with an admission of 80 pesos for adults. There is a cafeteria on site.

Xlapak

Our next stop is at the Mayan ruins of Xlapak, a short way down the peaceful road from Labná.

Masks of the Maya rain god Chaac at Xlapak.

The intricately carved stones at Xlapak are in a style unique to this area. We met a man some years ago that maintained that if you imbibed enough of the hallucinogenic seeds from the morning glory flowers that are prolific in the area that you too could envision this type of sculpture. He added that if you only ate four seeds, you would feel good, but if you took forty you would begin building pyramids—we never tried.

Sayil

Sayil.

Sayil is impressive and of a similar style of nearby Uxmal to which it is connected by a straight paved *sacbe* road as were all of the Mayan temple sites. The detritus strewn grounds give some idea of the many centuries of crumbling abandonment.

Back on our bicycles and a short way down the lovely and quiet paved road where the only sounds were birds chirping and the passing wind in our ears, we come to the Mérida-Campeche road.

The Mérida–Campeche bus in this photo passes several times a day. There is however no bus service along the *Ruta Puuc* road, which we had just traversed.

We spotted some shade and went to soak it up at the Yucatán–Campeche border inspection station. The friendly inspectors were from Mérida and proved to be jovial.

With a straight smooth road and a slight tail wind, Jane and I were doing at times 38 kilometers per hour heading north to Kabah. This is biking at its best.

Kabah

Kabah.

We would recommend that if you are interested in visiting these very impressive and lovely Mayan ruins that you spend the night in Santa Elena and bike to Kabah very early in the morning. This place is just too good to rush through. You can then leisurely enjoy this classic place and take pleasure in its exceptional artistic quality. You will be richly rewarded for your efforts with an unforgettable one of a kind memory.

Back in the jungle along a tropical forest path behind the main ruins of Kabah, Jane and I came to an interesting stand-alone building. One of the points of interest was the six meter deep unmarked hole alongside our path. Upon inspection we recognized it as one of the cisterns constructed by the ancient Mayan people to collect rain water in this area with no rivers, lakes or springs. While rereading *Incidents of Travel in Yucatan* by John Stephens, I came across this entry colorfully describing this nearly inconspicuous hole:

My first visit to this place was marked by a brilliant exploit on the part of my horse. On dismounting, Mr. Catherwood found shade for his horse, Doctor Cabot got his into one of the buildings, and I tied mine to this tree, giving him fifteen or twenty feet of halter as a range for pasture. Here we left them, but on our return in the evening my horse was missing, and, as we supposed, stolen; but before we reached the tree I saw the halter still attached to it, and I knew that an Indian would be much more likely to steal the halter and leave the horse than vice versa. The halter was drawn down into the mouth of a cave, and looking over the edge, I saw the horse hanging at the other end, with just rope enough, by stretching his head and neck, to keep a foothold at one side of the cave. One of his sides was scratched and grimed with dirt, and it seemed as if every bone in his body must be broken, but on getting him out we found that, except some scarifications of the skin, he was not at all hurt; in fact, he was quite the reverse, and never moved better than on our return to the village.

Fortunately we spotted the hole and our fate was better than that of John Stephen's horse.

Iguana at Kabah.

A giant iguana is one of many of Kabah's resident's whose ancestors have witnessed the arrival of the Maya, conquistadors, and now throngs of international jet-setters, and for him, not much will change.

On the smooth road from the Campeche–Mérida cut-off to Kabah and on to Santa Elena, you can sizzle along all the way. Jane started on her bike only a few seconds ahead of me, and she was just a small distant speck by the time I saddled up. I had to huff and puff to overtake her.

Next stop, Sacbe Bungalows.

Santa Elena

South of the city center of Santa Elena in a dense jungle setting is located Sacbe Bungalows, our lovely home base for the rest of our excursion in the area. These rustic immaculately clean cabins are cooled by the shade of a tropical forest and assisted by ceiling fans. Singing native birds and fragrant flowering plants make this our kind of place. It is quiet, tranquil, and convenient.

Santa Elena is out of the tourist loop and perfect headquarters for excursions into the Puuc with the Mayan ruins of Uxmal close at hand.

In the early 1840s the explorer John L. Stephens used Santa Elena, then known as Nohcacab, as a base from which he and his companions explored the Puuc region. In his book, *Incidents of Travel in Yucatan*, Stephens recorded accounts of the people of Nohcacab and their culture, and his associate Frederick Catherwood made drawings of the village and the region.

Church at Santa Elena.

At the front of the church, a long flight of stairs leads to the entrance, a stairway no doubt used since ancient times when the Maya worshiped their own gods at a temple that stood here.

Santa Elena has kept this small corner of town virtually unchanged over all these years. Stephens and Catherwood resided in the building on the east side of the church during their visit. Their apartment is now a museum that is worth a visit. The museum contains some mummified human remains, which some people speculate may be children of German colonists who settled here.

During the Second Mexican Empire (1864-1867) Germans established a colony, Villa Carlota, and some members of the colony resided in the town that is now Santa Elena, then on the front lines of the protracted Caste War. The colony failed. Events of the time were against the colony, and they were merely cannon fodder in the Caste War and a buffer against the warring Maya. Descendents of this colony remain today in Santa Elena and in Mérida. Alma Durán-Merk has written an intriguing book about Villa Carlota and that period of Mexican history; *Identifying Villa Carlota:*

German Settlements in Yucatán, México, During the Second Empire. The Spanish language version is *Villa Carlota,* available for sale at Sacbe Bungalows.

After a night at Sacbe Bungalows, we are off to an early start with savory scrumptious chicken tacos at a taco stand on the central plaza of Santa Elena before striking off to the Mayan ruins of Uxmal.

Sacbe Bungalows.

Uxmal

Drawing by Catherwood of House of the Dwarf, Uxmal.

The famous ruins of Uxmal and the temple, The House of the Dwarf, were drawn by Mr. Catherwood during his visit to Uxmal three-hundred years after the conquest of Yucatán by the Spanish.

Pictured above is the House of the Dwarf many years after Mr. Catherwood's visit. An interesting phenomenon here is the fact that if you clap your hands together in the place where Jane is standing, the echo loudly comes back off the ruins sounding like the crack of a rifle.

The temples and buildings at Uxmal took an astronomical amount of human effort to build, especially considering that no modern mechanical equipment was used. The restoration work alone presented a monumental amount of exertion.

Uxmal is an immense and impressive site. It would be exhaustive to present it all here and needless since it is well described in all guide books to the Yucatán Peninsula. I encourage you to come and take a look for yourself

Returning from Uxmal to Santa Elena on our bicycles, a view of the distant church of Santa Elena perched above the central plaza came into view just as John L. Stephens described in *Incidents of Travel in Yucatan*:

> *I was an hour crossing the sierra, and on the other side my first view of the great plain took in the church of Nohcacab (Santa Elena), standing like a colossus in the wilderness, the only token to indicate the presence of man. Descending the plain, I saw nothing but trees, until, when close upon the village, the great church again rose before me, towering above the houses, and the only object visible.*

We found Stephen's description of this place amazingly accurate, and the only noticeable change since 1840 when it was written was the fact that now there is a new paved and smooth road from Uxmal directly to Santa Elena. Even using our brakes prodigiously, we soon attained 40 kilometers of speed on our descent into Santa Elena.

We ended our day dining at the Pickled Onion, owned by Valerie Pickles. The Pickled Onion is located just a few meters from the entrance to the Sacbe Bungalows and is always a good choice for a snack or full meal. We opted for an order of delicious fajitas.

Side Trips from Santa Elena

From Santa Elena, there are many options for returning to Mérida. On this trip we rode north toward Mérida and home. We biked down out of the Puuc hills, through Ticul and north through the citrus country to Sacalum where we turned west to Abalá, and the road become a lot smaller. See Chapter 15, Sacalum–Citincabchén–Xcanchakan.

The option of taking the bus to Mérida directly from Ticul is a good choice. But before you board the bus consider the many eating options in Ticul.

Getting there:
TAME Bus Terminal - Mérida
Calle 69 between Calle 68 and 70

Santa Elena Lodging and Restaurants:

Sacbe Bungalows
Website: www.sacbebungalows.com.mx
Annette and Edgar are the owners of the most ecologically friendly accommodations to be found in Yucatán: Sacbe Bungalows. With over twenty years of dedicated involvement in keeping a balance of nature alive and well, they have established a harmony with the environment.

From their solar heated water system to the extensive collection of well marked and labeled trees, shrubs, and a cactus garden, the serenity is so complete it makes you want to whisper.

This place is not only bicycle friendly, it happens to be the perfect jumping off place for bike tours to Uxmal, Ticul, the

Mayan ruins of Kabah, Sayil, Labná, Loltún, and on to the Ruta Puuc hills with more Mayan ruins than you could visit in a season. The roads of the Puuc region are mostly quiet and well paved.

The Pickled Onion Restaurant and Cabins
The Pickled Onion is located on the hillside just outside Santa Elena on the road south to Kabah. The restaurant serves breakfast, lunch, and dinner, and offers their pool for a cooling dip. They also have Mayan style cabins for rent. Website: http://thepickledonionyucatan.com

Related chapters:
Chapter 3, Oxkutzcab
Chapter 9, Ticul
Chapter 12, Yaxhachen – Oxkutzcab to Tekax
Chapter 13, Tekax
Chapter 15, Sacalum–Citincabchén–Xcanchakan

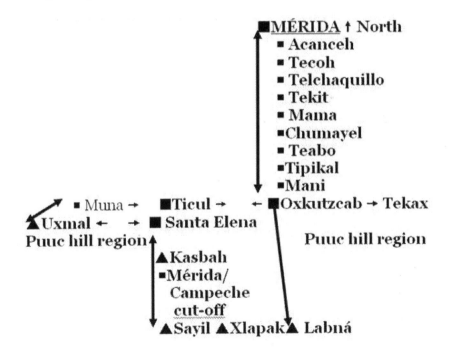

Chapter 15

Sacalum–Citincabchén–Xcanchakan

Each time a driver makes a trip by cycle instead of by automobile, not only the cyclist but society as a whole reaps the benefits. Marcia D. Lowe

We began this bike ride in Santa Elena, biking down out of the Puuc hills passing through Ticul, and then north through the citrus country to Sacalum where we turned east and the road became perceptively smaller.

Sacalum has the fortress church of San Antonio. It sits high up on a rock above the town. This church was establish here as an Indian chapel in the mid 1500's and a hundred years later the church that stands today was completed.

In Sacalum, we had two choices of roads. One would take us on to Mucuyché and Abalá and the other to Citincabchén. We turned back to the direction we had come, turned east at the sign for Citincabchén, and the road became considerably less significant the further we went.

Neglected and nearly forgotten by the world, Citincabchén was in its heyday one of the highest production henequen plantations (*haciendas*) in Yucatán. Boat loads of Korean workers were brought in on contract to work in the henequen fields.

The ruins of the Citincabchén hacienda.

Today Citincabchén has but one claim to fame, and it is the product of a tortilla shop that turned out the best tortillas of our trip and perhaps as good as we have ever had...worth the trip just to sample. When we purchased our tortillas we were offered a bag of *kimchi*. This is a traditional Korean dish of fermented cabbage with vegetables and hot peppers. The Korean community is still actively involved in Yucatán and even sponsors a free children's medical facility in Mérida.

This outpost of civilization is money poor but rich in clean fresh air and tranquility.

Down the road we continue to slip into a seldom visited realm of motorless silence. We passed through the town of Hunabchén, and then our narrow paved road turned into a narrow rocky lane that we hoped would lead us to our final destination of Xcanchakan.

This rock strewn six kilometer stretch of road took us an hour and a half to transit—we did some walking.

Rough trail.

At a bad spot along the trail I said to Jane, "It can't get any worse", but it did! Jane called the road *camino feo* or ugly road in English. We did meet other travelers on this stretch, and they had this to say when we inquired as to how much further to a good road; "*No es lejos*" and "*falta poco*" or "it is not far" and "just a little further". This little six kilometer stretch of road took more out of us than the 57 kilometers that we had already biked that morning from Santa Elena. The rough road ended in the small Mayan village of Mahzucil.

In our explorations of Mahzucil, we met a man bedecked with his shotgun, machete, and belt loaded with shells. He was on his way out into the woods in search of wild game that included deer, turkey, wild boar, and anything big enough to warrant the cost of a shotgun shell. When we told him we were looking for a place to eat he took us to his home, which was only accessible by a footpath into the jungle.

The hunter of Mahzucil,

We were treated to delicious turkey *salbutes* prepared over the wood fire in a centuries old tradition of the Maya.

When we asked what the tab would be we were told there was no charge, and they meant it, but we gave generously and thanked them ever so much for their open and friendly hospitality.

Mahzucil Mayan kitchen.

A Mexican stand-off!

On our road to Xcanchakan, cattle blocked our way. Some had horns and looked dangerous to me. I am no expert on this kind of confrontation, but I know that tranquility accompanied by very slow movements sets the pace for their actions. We waited to be accepted and allowed the occupants of our passage way to exit the road at their own unhurried leisurely pace. We were definitely outnumbered and outweighed.

We biked on to our next stop at Xcanchakan. A majestic hacienda was established here by the Spanish in 1542 on the land of the former Mayan city of Mayapán.

The book *Incidents of Travel in Yucatan* by John L. Stephens aroused our interest in Xcanchakan. In the book, Stephens gives an interesting description of it, and his partner Frederick Catherwood did an engraving that was positively fascinating—we just had to visit the place.

Hacienda Xcanchakan by Frederick Catherwood,1840.

One hundred and eighty years later the Hacienda Xcanchakan is little changed outwardly. This is the view that greeted us upon our arrival at the hacienda.

Hacienda Xcanchakan had the unique distinction of being one of the very first *encomiendas* awarded to the recently arrived Spanish conquistadors and actually predated the city of Mérida by two years. Initially the hacienda produced Indian corn and cattle.

When Stephens and Catherwood arrived at this spot back in 1840, the sugar industry was just beginning, henequen production hadn't yet begun, and the sixty year Caste War was only a fermenting time bomb waiting to explode, and Yucatán was considering the status of an independent country.

Before the arrival of the Spaniards, this location had been one of the largest of the Mayan cities with more than 4,000 stone structures that encompassed the adjacent beautiful Mayan city of Mayapán. See Chapter 1.

At the village center cross roads you can still view what remains of one of the many Mayan temples, which have been severely looted for building materials to construct the hacienda and church.

Xcanchakan − A bull ring is under construction in preparation for a festival in honor of Santo Niño Dios.

Xcanchakan is not only rural but totally out of the path of visiting tourists and has no hotels or restaurants though it is possible to have a meal prepared for you in the home of Doña Adela Navarro. Doña Adela has no phone and her address is *domicilio conocido* or her address is known, but, you must ask around. Everyone knows her.

When we arrived in Xcanchakan, the festival in honor of Santo Niño Dios was under way in this underprivileged town. At the church service there was hardly a single person who arrived with a motor vehicle. There was one exception to the motor vehicle scenario, and that was the priest who arrived in a chrome bedecked late model automobile.

Festival in honor of Santo Niño Dios, Xcanchakan.

After the service the congregation took to the street to parade through the town. They were accompanied by a rag-tag musical group blasting earsplitting out-of-tune notes and led by a slightly inebriated pyrotechnic who positively delighted in sending his smoking skyrockets blasting into backyards where they expired in reverberating explosions.

Jane and I were the only two tourists in attendance at the Xcanchakan traditional fiesta.

John in Xcanchakan.

Xcanchakan streets were built for single file carriages, and they haven't been upgraded since.

Waiting for the bus to Mérida.

Two buses and several *colectivo* taxis make the round trip journey from Mérida down the quiet three meter wide road to Hacienda Xcanchakan each day. We had a choice to wait an hour for the Mérida bus or to bike to the next village of Telchaquillo where bus service to Mérida is more frequent. We opted for Telchaquillo.

Mayan women on their way to the *molino* to have their boiled corn ground for tortillas.

In distance this trip is not far, but in time reference it is a quantum leap back to centuries gone by.

Getting there from Mérida

Santa Elena and Ticul
TAME bus terminal
Calle 69 between Calle 68 and 70

Xcanchacan and Telchaquillo
Noreste bus terminal
Calle 67 near the corner of Calle 50

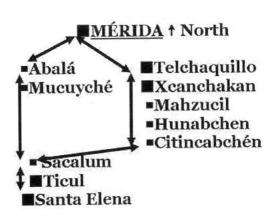

Chapter 16

Telchaquillo, Pixya, Sabacché Cenote Route

Bike and Bus Day Trip

Telchaquillo is a small Mayan village nearly forgotten by the passing years where most of the inhabitants speak Yucatec Maya.

This is definitely not a tourist crossroads with sophisticated glitter and glitz enticing advertisements beckoning visitors to hang out here. It is, however, close to the Mayan ruins of Mayapán, and little changed over the centuries.

In the city center is a deep *cenote* with a staircase leading all the way down to water level, eight meters below the surface. A low wall around the top keeps pedestrian mishaps to a minimum.

Telchaquillo church.

Across the street from the *cenote* is a modest unkempt no frills church that doesn't even have a paved walkway to its front door. We were told that the church is built over a large *cenote*. Mayan stone carvings taken from nearby ruins have been used to decorate the facade.

Even with the sad state of this impoverished little village, a carnival company had hauled in amusement rides in order to ring a few *centavos* out of this hard pressed hardscrabble economy.

There aren't any restaurants in Telchaquillo, but there is almost always a lady selling fruit at the corner where the bus to Mérida stops, and across the street is a store where the owner will make you a sandwich.

Fruit seller in Telchaquillo.

Pixya

We came back to Telchaquillo to make a side trip. On a previous visit we spotted a sign pointing to Pixya. We had never heard of Pixya but being curious we soon had our map out and discovered a small road leading to Pixya from Telchaquillo, and then from Pixya a trail leading to Sabacché and on to Tekit. We just had to bike this road.

We took an early morning bus to Telchaquillo and set out to explore, not knowing where our day would end.

We set off on our bikes on the road to Pixya.

The ruins of a hacienda in Pixya.

At the end of the pavement at the seldom visited silent Mayan village of Pixya, we found the ruins of a neglected hacienda. Pixya in Yucatec Maya means wounded knee.

Biking east from little Pixya we met a man who volunteered to guide us across the narrow lane out of Pixya that led to our next destination, the *cenote* of Sabacché. Armed with a machete and a 16 gauge single shot shotgun, our guide, Manual Chable, was always on the alert for wild game to feed his family.

Our route led us through scant low scrub jungle that was vigorously harvested for its meager wood supply. The wood is used for home cooking because of the prohibitively high cost of LP gas.

One of the few indications of man's presence on our five kilometer track across the *sacbe* road was a cemetery surrounded by a wall. The ten by twenty meter cemetery compound spoke volumes about the impoverished inhabitants, and wreaked an unmistakable breath robbing stench of decomposition that cut through the fresh flower scented air like a blast of foul malodorous death.

Manual Chable and Jane on the trail to Sabacché.

Manual Chable, our Mayan jungle guide, left us at the newly constructed palm thatched pavilion overlooking the Sabacché *cenote* where we rested in the shade. The sun was getting hot. We decided to turn back to Telchaquillo for a bus to Mérida. We knew the bus from Sabacché to Mérida had already passed through town.

On the return trip, I followed a small jungle path off the road and came across a ten meter deep *cenote* with dangerously steep stone walls that could easily trap an unobservant jungle stroller.

If you fell into that *cenote* and managed to survive your fall, your chances of rescue would be slim to none in this sparsely populated place.

Nearly everything that survives in this semiarid jungle scrub has spines and stickers. A kilometer from Pixya on our return trip one of those spines punctured my tire. Luck was with us because the only motor vehicle we saw all morning materialized heading our way and transported me and my deflated tire into the little village of Pixya. The truck, which was loaded with charcoal, was just returning from a week in the forest making charcoal. The truck dropped me at the humble abode of the Ku Puch family where assistance was attempted.

The Pixya bicycle shop.

In the front yard of the Ku Puch family an amazing variety of curiosities are found. First, it became a bicycle repair shop where a patch was applied to the spine puncture wound on my tire. The rock barren yard is also the kitchen of the Puch family where they cook over an open wood fire using three stones and a refrigerator grate. Six mangy mutts of questionable pedigree struggled to rouse themselves when we all arrived. They slowly sauntered aside while the repair job got under way. The electric service entrance was fastened to a worm eaten wooden pole where the bare wires have no conduit protection, and, of course, no ground wire.

All of the heroic efforts to repair my bicycle tire were to no avail when the tire blew out after I had traveled less than one-hundred meters, leaving the tube ruptured beyond further repair. We were all saddened by the turn of events.

I got a ride to Telchaquillo with another truck while Jane biked behind. In Telchaquillo we searched the town for a replacement tube but found none.

Plan "B" was to catch the bus back to Mérida, which we did.

Our little folding bicycles make public transportation wonderfully fun and easy because we can board any bus or *colectivo* taxi that comes along, and they are frequent here.

Getting there:
Noreste Bus Terminal – Mérida
Calle 67 near the corner of Calle 50

■MÉRIDA ↑ North   (40 km Mérida to Telchaquillo)

■Acanceh
■Tecoh
■**Telchaquillo** →   ■**Pixya**→   ■**Sabacché** (Cenote route)

Chapter 17

Motul Day Trip

An easy day trip from Mérida

This ancient Mayan city, originally known as *Zacmotul*, is just 40 kilometers east of Mérida, and is an easy bus ride that takes you on a scenic route through a number of small towns.

San Juan Bautista of Motul.

The centerpiece of Motul is its massive church, site of one of the earliest Franciscan monasteries in Yucatán. The monastery contains a very unusual colonial mural from the late 1700s that features a clock-like calendar wheel. The fresco is in red, blue and ocher.

Motul was the birthplace to the popular 1920s socialist governor Felipe Carrillo Puerto. Felipe Carrillo Puerto's home and birth place are here in an unpretentious dwelling that is today a museum dedicated to his life, political career, and socialist movement. Governor Carrillo Puerto championed the rights of the indigenous Mayan of Yucatán with land reforms and workers' rights.

Monument to Felipe Carrillo Puerto stands in the central plaza of Motul.

A brief look at the history surrounding Felipe Carrillo Puerto

The governor of Yucatán from 1915-1918, a former Mexican military man, Salvador Alvarado, laid the ground work for a socialist-populist movement that brought in a very popular social reformer named Felipe Carrillo Puerto.

After México's nearly three hundred years of slavery, the Mexican-American War, the Yucatán fight for sovereignty, the protracted Caste War that begun in 1847, the turbulent revolutionary war that lasted about ten years ultimately brought about social reform.

Felipe Carrillo Puerto was elected as governor of Yucatán with a platform of workers' rights, land reform and equality for the indigenous Mayan people.

Elected in 1922, Felipe became governor and instituted many social reforms in Yucatán. However, political and military power from other parts of Mexico turned against him, and he was arrested, and then executed along with thirteen companions, three of them his brothers, at the Mérida cemetery by a firing squad on January 3, 1924. His last words were "No *abandonéis a mis indios*" (Do not abandon my Indians).

This is the monument and crypt of Felipe Carrillo Puerto at the main cemetery in Mérida, Yucatán. Here also are entombed three of the brothers of Felipe, and a number of other socialist leaders of the state.

If there is one thing that we really liked about little Motul, it was that like in many European countries people rode bicycles to work, school, and market.

Easy bike parking is adjacent to the market and city hall.

Around the central park, horse drawn taxis called *calesas* are not tourist rides but ground transport for local shoppers.

This is exactly how Mérida looked years ago with *calesa* taxis and no stop lights before the onset of its population explosion that brought the population of Mérida from 175,000 in 1972 to nearly a million today.

There is definitely something positive to be said for a quiet slow unhurried pace of life like Motul still enjoys today.

In the municipal market on the wall is an old stone cut coat of arms that depicts the city's original Mayan name of *Zacmotul*.

In Motul's city center are the old and new. The nearly five hundred year old church–monastery complex and the microwave tower stand together. In Mexico, where now nearly everyone is busily chatting by cellular phones, microwave towers have sprung up everywhere.

It is possible to make the trip to and from Motul by bicycle but the road traffic is congested. Bus and taxi service to Mérida is frequent.

Taking a bus or *colectivo* taxi gives more relaxing time in town to see the sights, visit the market and enjoy Motul's culinary claim to fame, *motuleños*—you must try them!

Getting there:
Noreste Bus Terminal – Mérida
Calle 67 between Calle 50 and 52

Chapter 18

Aké Archeological Site

Visit Tixkokob, famous for its hammocks

John taking in the view from the top of a temple at Aké.

Aké is a small tranquil Mayan archeological site and village located 32 kilometers east of Mérida. An excursion to Aké makes a lovely bike–bus–taxi day trip where you will be treated to a rare commodity in this day and time.

Believe it or not, at Aké there are absolutely no tour buses, trinket vending peddlers, hammock hawkers, or glitzy accommodations. This is the main attraction for those that want to experience a small slice of vintage Yucatán off the beaten tourist path.

The ruins of Aké are a striking anomaly amongst the entire collection of Mayan ruins of Mexico and Central America. They are inconsistent with the scale and proportions found elsewhere. Here you will find colossal steps built for giants.

Another interesting feature of the ruins of Aké is the network of straight Mayan roads known as *sacbe*. They were originally paved with white stucco. The *sacbeob* tied the ancient empire of the Mayan civilization together. Though now mostly overgrown by jungle vegetation, the Mayan *sacbe* road from Aké to the adjacent ruins of Izamal, some twenty-five kilometers, is still viably existent, and only lacks clearing to make it usable again. This road originated at Mérida, formerly known as T'ho, and ran all the way to the Caribbean coast a distance of nearly three hundred kilometers. Over the years Jane and I have encountered numerous Mayan roads, and we have actually driven on some of them.

To reach Aké we bicycled from our home in Mérida to the city center where we boarded a *colectivo* taxi and rode to the town of Tixkokob, famous for their hammocks. From Tixkokob we biked to Aké.

In addition to the Mayan ruins at Aké, there is an old henequen processing operation open for tours, a small 1500s chapel, and colonial buildings, which make the seldom visited site a worthwhile side trip.

We first visited the henequen mill of Aké in 1986. Little has changed since. This facility continues to turn out their end product of sisal fiber used primarily for baling twine and other rope products.

This facility was originally powered by a gigantic diesel engine with two cylinders. The engine blew up and sent an employee through the roof, skyrocketing his body all the way to the adjacent Mayan pyramid where it came to its earthly landing. A cross was erected at that spot to commemorate his suborbital flight.

Twenty-five years ago that cross was still standing on the pyramid, but the two cylinder diesel engine was reduced to one cylinder that was ingeniously still sputtering along at about sixty unsteady revolutions per minute and powering contrivances that somehow took the green sharp pointed agave's leaves and converted them to sisal fiber.

The old diesel engine finally sputtered its last sputter, and now the antiquated rusty and worn old machinery is powered by electric motors.

One thing that has not changed since the beginning of operations here more than a century ago is the system of tiny railway tracks and horse drawn gondolas that quietly and efficiently transport the materials around the hacienda.

Be sure to bring your camera because this is photo-op country at its best.

Getting there:
Colectivo taxi from Mérida to Tixkokob
Calle 54a between Calle 65 and 67
Departs every 30 minutes starting at 5:30 a.m.

Centro Bus Terminal – Mérida
Calle 65 between Calle 46 and 48
next to "Casa del Pueblo" in downtown Mérida.

■MÉRIDA ↑ North (38 km Mérida to Aké)

 ■ **Tixkokob** →   ■Cacalchén
↓
▲ Aké

Get a bicycle. You will not regret it if you live. ~Mark Twain

Chapter 19

Buses and Colectivo Taxis

You haven't seen the real Yucatán until you bike and bus it

Buses and Bus Terminals of Mérida, Yucatán

The intention of this chapter is to assist those adventurers and bicyclers who wish to incorporate bus/taxi transport into their travel adventures in and out of Mérida.

First class and luxury buses will definitely get you there fast and efficiently, but for fun, excitement, and adventure, second class will take you to the places that tourists miss most. They travel to the out of the way villages where you will meet the people that live there. Second class buses stop on demand, and take longer than first class buses, and they are perfect for eccentric penny pinchers.

The following information does <u>not</u> give a complete list of all the destinations that the numerous Mérida bus companies service. However, that current information can be found by visiting the websites or calling the listed telephone numbers.

Not all buses have space for full-sized bicycles. Folding bicycles that are folded are best because they will go on or in all buses and *colectivo* taxis (vans), and even if there is no storage space below or luggage rack on top, many will accommodate your bicycle inside. You might have to buy an extra seat for the displaced space.

Full-sized bikes usually can be stowed below in the baggage compartment on first class buses and on the second class bus lines of Mayab and Orienté. There is sometimes a charge for a bicycle. On second class buses, the driver decides if you pay and on first class buses, the baggage handler will decide if there is an additional fee for a bicycle in the luggage compartment.

CAME bus terminal - Centro de autobuses Mérida

Calle 70 between Calle 69 and 71
Downtown Mérida
Tel. 999-924-8391, 923-4440, 923-4443
Lines: ADO, ADO-GL and Platino
www.ado.com.mx

CAME bus terminal - *Centro de autobuses Mérida.*

The Platino buses are fabulous; they have extra wide fully reclining luxury seats, his and hers rest rooms, and a wet bar with coffee, tea, bottled water, and soft drinks included. A kit containing ear plugs, ear buds, eye covers, plus a pillow and blanket are standard equipment. Many people ride these buses though the night and save the price of a hotel room.

Destinations from CAME: Cancún, Campeche, Ciudad Del Carmen, Cordoba, Playa del Carmen, Chetumal, Tulum, Veracruz, Minatitlán, E. Zapata, Palenque, Puebla, México City, Valladolid, Ocosingo, Tuxtla-Gtz, Chichén Itzá, San Cristobal de las Casas, and Belize City, Belize.

ADO operates most of the first class buses, which include Platino and GL. They have the best quality and set the standard for all Mexican buses. You will always see these buses professionally driven, and in good condition.

Mérida Fiesta Americana
Across Calle 60 from the Hotel Fiesta Americana in Plaza Bonita
Calle 60 and Av. Colón
Tel. 999-925-0910
Lines: ADO-GL, Platino plus Cancún Airport van
Destinations: Cancún, Cancún Airport, and Villahermosa.

Mérida Alta Brisas
Alta Brisas Mall
Avenida Racho Correa
Near Star Medica
Lines: ADO-GL, Platino plus Cancún Airport van
Destinations: Cancún, Cancún Airport.

TAME – Terminal de Autobuses Mérida
Calle 69 between Calles 68 and 70
Downtown

TAME bus terminal - Terminal de Autobuses Mérida.
This is where you will find what is called the economical buses, plus the first class bus to Chetumal, Clase Europea. It leaves from this terminal at 10 a.m., 4 p.m, 10:30 p.m., and midnight. The trip takes 5 ½ hours. The Clase Europea bus

has toilets, but most of the buses leaving from this terminal do not.

TAME is also where you will find; OCC, Mayab, ATS, Oriente, and TRT bus lines. This is where you find the Mayab buses that go to Ticul, Oxkutzcab and Tekax.

Buses from here run to the Caribbean coast, all over Yucatán, Campeche and Tabasco. Here you find the buses to Uxmal and Holbox. Also, you can buy tickets here for all the ADO buses, although they leave from the CAME terminal, which is around the corner on Calle 70.

Terminal Autobuses del Noreste, Oriente and Lus
Calle 67 between Calle 50 and 52
Near the corner with Calle 50
Tel. 999 924 6355 and 923 0548

Terminal Autobuses del Noreste, Oriente and Lus.

These buses are all second class, meaning that they have no on-board toilet facilities, and stop anywhere on demand.

This is the best terminal to use for day trips that will take you off the main roads to quaint villages and old haciendas. Buses from this station run to the beautiful Mayan ruins of Mayapán. If you buy a ticket to Mayapán, make sure you specify the ruins of Mayapán (*ruinas de Mayapán or zona archeologica de Mayapán*) or you may end up in the village of Mayapán many kilometers from the archeological site of the same name.

Folding bicycles are no charge, but, they have a tight fit in the small luggage compartments under these buses.

The Autobuses del Noreste ticket counter also sells ADO tickets to all destinations in Mexico.

Three bus lines are here: Noreste, Oriente and Lus. Destinations from Mérida on Noreste line and Oriente are Celestún, Motul, Izamal, Espita, Hunucmá, Sisal,Dzidzantún, Dzilám Gonzales, Dzilám de Bravo, Buctzotz, Tizimín, Rio Lagartos, San Felipe, Kantunikin, Valladolid, and Cancún, and more.

From Mérida on the Lus line; Acanceh, Tecoh, Teabo, Chumayel, Tekit, Mamá, Maní, Oxkutzcab, Peto, Cuzamá, Homún and Huhí, and more.

Terminal del Centro - Centro Autobuses
Calle 65 between 46 and 48
Next to *Casa del Pueblo* in downtown Mérida.
Tel. 923 9962, 923 9941 extension 15

Terminal del Centro - Centro Autobuses.

Destinations from Mérida on Centro Autobuses: These buses head towards Valladolid and Cancun with many stops along the way, including Tixkokob, and Izamal. Centro also has buses to Motul.

These second class buses have no on-board toilet facilities, and make frequent stops. The equipment is well maintained, and their departures are frequent.

Autoprogreso - Progreso Bus Terminal
Calle 62 No. 524 between Calle 65 and 67
Downtown Mérida   Tel. 999-928-3965
Website: www.autoprogreso.com/

Autoprogreso - Progreso Bus Terminal.

Autoprogreso has comfortable, airconditioned buses that depart about every 20 minutes between 5 a.m. and 10:30 p.m. from their terminal in Mérida on Calle 62 located between Calle 65 and 67. Buses out of this station also serve the beach towns of Chuburná Puerto and Chelém.

Vans - *Colectivo taxis* or *Combis*

These fast moving multi-passenger vans park on the street or have terminals at numerous designated spots in downtown Mérida, near and around the main municipal market and also in the Parque San Juan located between Calle 62 and Calle 64 and Calle 69a in downtown Mérida.

There are *colectivo* taxis to almost all villages in Yucatán.

Most *colectivo* taxis take departure when they have sufficient passengers.

The nice thing about these *colectivo* taxis is that you can flag them down anywhere, and they are numerous throughout Yucatán. So, returning to Mérida is quick and easy. We often times bus out to our biking area, and then we return by *colectivo* taxi, which will get you back to Mérida fast.

Taxi terminal for Tekax located on Calle 62 near Calle 69a, Parque San Juan in downtown Mérida.

Above are numerous *colectivo* taxis parked near the main market on Calle 67 near the corner of Calle 54. The first one is from Mérida to Acanceh and Tecoh.

The vans will stop anywhere, but full sized bicycles could be a problem unless you find a taxi with a roof-top rack, and in that case the sky is the limit. Expect to pay an extra fare for your bike if it is loaded top-side. Almost all of these taxis have room for a couple of folding bicycles inside behind the rear seats. They rarely charge extra for the folding bikes.

The possibility of end destinations with these *colectivo* taxis is extensive.

You haven't seen the real Yucatán until you bike and bus it.

After more than a quarter century of doing these excursions, we still have a long list of end-destinations to explore.

What are you waiting for? Come on and have the adventure of a lifetime.

It is curious that with the advent of the automobile and the airplane, the bicycle is still with us. Perhaps people like the world they can see from a bike, or the air they breathe when they're out on a bike... Or because they like the feeling of being able to hurtle through air one minute, and saunter through a park the next, without leaving behind clouds of choking exhaust, without leaving behind so much as a footstep. ~Gurdon S. Leete

Excerpted from *The Quotable Cyclist: Great Moments of Bicycling Wisdom, Inspiration and Humor* by Bill Strickland.

Bilingual Glossary of Terms

Mayan = (m) Spanish = (sp)

Agua oxigenada (sp) hydrogen peroxide.

Auto de Fe (sp) In 1478 King Ferdinand and Queen Isabella had received permission from Pope Sixtus IV to name Inquisitors throughout their domain, to protect Catholicism as the true faith. They immediately began establishing permanent trials and developing bureaucracies to carry out investigations. Franciscan missionaries brought the Inquisition to the Yucatán. A major aspect of the tribunals was the *auto de fe* religious ceremony. In July 1562, Friar Diego de Landa held an *auto de fe* Inquisitional ceremony in Maní, burning a number of Maya books and 5000 idols, saying that they were "works of the devil." This act and numerous incidents of torture at the monastery were used to speed the mass adoption of Catholicism throughout the region.

Botanas (sp) Snacks.

Cal (sp) Hydrated lime.

Calabasa (sp) Name to several varieties of squash grown, and harvested for their seeds. The seeds are used in a wide variety of ways in Mayan cooking.

Calesa (sp) Open horse drawn carriage used for taxi or touring.

Callejeros (sp) Street dogs.

Campesino (sp) Country man.

Can sacbe (m) Mayan word meaning road of snakes.

Carnival, A week long pre-lent/Easter festival of parades, street dancing, noise making and beer drinking with roots in a prehistoric pagan spring celebration. Mérida has the second largest event in Mexico. The world's largest carnival is in Brazil with New Orleans being the largest in the United States. (carnaval = Spanish/ English = carnival)

Carretera (sp) A major highway or road.

Caste War, guerra de las castas (sp) A protracted battle between the Yucatec Maya and Spanish colonialists of

Yucatán known as the *Guerra de las castas*. Begun in 1847, this conflict ultimately divided the Yucatán peninsula into Campeche state, Yucatán state and the Territory of Quintana Roo.

Caste War Route. The road to visiting the towns and places affected in the Caste War.

Cenotes (sp) Derived from the Mayan Dzonot. In Yucatán a *cenote* is a sinkhole formed in the rock strata that exposes water to the surface. **Zona de Cenotes** (sp) Area with numerous sinkholes.

Cerros, (sp) In Yucatán, over grown Mayan ruin mounds are referred to as *cerros* or hills.

Chaltune (m) Mayan cistern for the collection of rain water.

Chan Santa Cruz Indians. They were also known as the **Cruzob** Maya. These were separatist Maya of the Caste War era who established their own territory, religion and capital city in the isolated jungle. Their capital in the jungle, Chan Santa Cruz, was the site of a Mayan temple named Balam-Na, or House of the Jaguar Priest. It was built using labor of captive white prisoners of the Caste War. Chan Santa Cruz was overrun by Mexican federal troops in 1901, and occupied until the Mexicans capitulated in 1915, marking the longest Indian insurgency in the Americas.

Chilam Balam of Chumayel. The so-called books of Chilam Balam are handwritten in the Yucatec language using the Latin alphabet. They are named after the towns where they were originally kept. The book of the Chilam Balam of Chumayel is a late 18th-century manuscript copy of a Yucatec Maya chronicle, written and illustrated in Chumayel, Yucatán. The text records the Spanish conquest of the Yucatán, and provides information about the prophecy of Chilam Balam, the calendar, astronomy, creation of the world, rituals, and other subjects.

Ciclopista (sp) Bicycle path.

Ciénega (sp) Coastal lagoons.

Cocina económica (sp) An inexpensive restaurant usually run by one or two women. It is sometimes located in their home. It is open for the midday meal. Two or three different Yucatecan dishes are offered each day. All meals come with tortillas and usually soup or rice, and are always accompanied by the Yucatecan sizzling habanero chili sauce. You can order a full portion or half a portion. Take out is almost always available.

Codice (sp) Old manuscript dealing with noteworthy points of antiquity.

Colectivo taxi (sp) In Yucatán these are vans that circulate like buses. They travel fast and will stop anywhere to pick up passengers, if they have room.

Colonial In Yucatán, colonial can refer to the type of building construction; Spanish or French, or it can refer to a town or village established at the time when Mexico was a colony of Spain.

Comal (sp) Name of cooking utensil made of tin or pottery used over a wood fire. It is painted white with **cal** or hydrated lime to keep the food from sticking. It is principally used for making tortillas.

Copal (sp) Pitchy resinous wood burned in Mayan ceremonies to yield a distinctive aroma.

Corbel (sp) Name given to a type of arch used in ancient Mayan construction. It is not a true arch.

Cult of the Talking Cross. During the Caste War many Maya rejected the faith of the conquistadors, and established their own religion that was an amalgamation of the ancient Mayan and Catholicism. An off shoot of this cult religion is active to this day and is referred to as the *cult de la Santisimo Cruz*.

Dia de los Muertos (sp) Day of the Dead, a Mexican national holiday with area variations. A holiday festival observed with religious connotations and subdued partying that is not morbid. Graves are visited, decorated, and picnicking is done with a traditional chicken stuffed cornbread called *pan de muerto* or bread of the dead. In Yucatán the event is held October 30- 31, and November 1-2, and Mayan tradition is commingled with Spanish custom. It is common to see special decorated altars with ceremonial events in area restaurants and private homes across Yucatán. Brightly colored little sugar skull candies are traditional.

Dicho (sp) A saying. For example; *pueblo chico, inferno grande* or small town, big hell.

Domicilio conocido (sp) Address is known. In small communities where the houses are not numbered and/or have no names for the streets, a person's mailing or delivery address would be their name plus *domicilio conocido*.

Dorado (sp) Golden.

El Laberinto (sp) The labyrinth.

El Pensamiento (sp) The Thinker.

Encomienda (sp) Land awarded as payment to Spanish mercenaries: a system that was employed by the Spanish crown during the colonization of the Americas. In the *encomienda*, the Spanish crown granted a person a specified number of natives for whom they were to take responsibility. In theory, the receiver of the grant was to protect the natives from warring tribes, and to instruct them in the Spanish language, and in the Catholic faith: in return they could extract tribute from the natives in the form of labor, gold or other products. In practice, the difference between *encomienda* and slavery could be minimal. Natives were forced to do strenuous labor and subjected to extreme punishment and death if they resisted.

Faro (sp) Lighthouse.

Folkloric dances. The traditional dance and music of Yucatán is the Jarana. The Jarana dates back at least two centuries and is strongly influenced by the indigenous Maya culture. The traditional dress of the Yucatecan Jarana is the *terno*, a huipil made of white cotton and decorated with colorful embroidered flowers. The simple dress of the male Jarana dancer is the white *guayabera* or *filipino* shirt, white pants, a red handkerchief hung from the belt, a Panama hat, and a pair of white sandals, known as *caclis*.

Frijol con puerco (sp) A meal made with black beans and pork traditionally eaten on a Monday in Yucatán. Do not confuse this with any canned products from north of the border. This is a gourmet delight.

Grutas (sp) Caves.

Guayaberas (sp) Traditional Yucatecan dress shirt.

Habanero (sp) Extremely hot chili pepper common in Yucatán, not believed to be indigenous. In the markets, the ladies selling these peppers cover their hands with a plastic bag when handling them.

Haciendas (sp) In Yucatán, a large landed estate. The hacienda originated in the Spanish colonial period and survived into the 20th century. The Maya were theoretically free wage earners on haciendas, but in practice their employers were able to bind them to the land, primarily by keeping them in a state of perpetual indebtedness. By the 19th century, as much as half of Mexico's rural population was entangled in the peonage system. Many haciendas were broken up by the Mexican Revolution (1910-1923).

Hamaca (sp) Hammock. The majority of people in Yucatán sleep in hammocks. Hammocks were developed and employed in the Americas before the arrival of the Spanish conquistadors, and continue to be made and used widely throughout Yucatán to this day. The most comfortable Yucatecan hammocks use nylon strings for their end sections but cotton for the main body.

Horchata (sp) A sweetened rice drink served cold or over ice.

Huevos a la Mexicana (sp) Huevos a la Mexicana are scrambled eggs cooked with chopped *serrano* chilies, onions, and tomatoes. They are served with refried beans and hot tortillas.

Huevos Motuleños (sp) A savory Yucatecan breakfast creation is built of toasted tortillas covered with refried black beans, fried eggs, tangy tomato sauce, green peas, chopped ham and grated fresh cheese accompanied by French bread to soak up the sauce and golden fried bananas. This dish originated in the town of Motul, thus motuleños meaning from Motul.

Huinic (m) **El Huinic**. He is a typical Mayan field worker who has tended the farmlands of Yucatán for countless centuries. A day's ration of water is carried in the gourd at his waist and a bag containing his pozol, cooked corn dough. He will mix the pozol with water and some chili peppers for his day's sustenance. The traditional garb consists of a small brim straw hat, white shirt, trousers rolled up to his knees, simple flat sandals of henequen twine, cloth pouch and water gourd hung from his waist. His universal cutting tool shaped like a hook is called a *coá*.

Huipil (sp) Also spelled **hipil**. A white smock type dress richly adorned with hand embroidery and worn over a lace trimmed slip. It is the traditional dress of indigenous Mayan women.

Jamaica (sp) Hibiscus tea.

Jefe (sp) Boss.

Jipi (sp) Local name given by the people of Becal, Campeche, to the palm and the palm fibers, which are woven to make Panama hats.

Kilómetro (sp) Kilometer. A kilometer is 1000 meters or .62 statue miles.

Lavabo mano (sp) Hand washing sink.

Legua (sp) A league (*legua*) is officially three miles or 4.8 kilometers. Here in Yucatán there is no official equivalent. The Maya reckon one league to be the distance a person can walk in one hour, and that will depend upon whether this is on a good flat road or through awful terrain.

Leña (sp) Wood cut for cooking fires.

Maiz (sp) Corn.

Masa (sp) Corn that has been boiled with lime and then ground into dough.

Maseca (sp) Dried masa to which water is added to make corn dough for tortillas.

Mayab (m) Yucatán.

Mestiza (sp) In Yucatán, a county woman who dresses in a huipil is called a *mestiza*.

Mestizo (sp) In Mexico, a person of mixed cultural heritage.

Metate (sp) A carved flat stone used by the ancient Maya to grind corn using a *mano,* a round cylinder shaped stone rolled over the corn that was placed on the surface of the *metate.*

Milpa (sp) A cornfield or plot of land worked by an indigenous farmer.

Molcajete (sp) A stone mortar and pestle used for grinding chilies, spices and herbs.

Molino (sp) A place where corn is taken to be ground by a machine.

Mosquitero (sp) A mosquito net used to cover a bed or hammock.

Nixtamal, **nixtamalizado**. (sp) Nixtamalization is the process of cooking corn with lime, which provides for the release of niacin into the diet. Beans, when consumed with corn that has been *nixtamalizado* provides the amino acids required to balance the diet for protein.

Nopal (sp) Prickly pear cactus. The young tender leaves are used in the cuisine of Mexico.

Palapa (sp) Mayan thatched roof home also called a *choza.*

Paletas (sp) Popsicles made of fresh fruits and juices.

Panaderia (sp) Bakery.

Panuchos (sp) **Buut 'bil bu'ul waaj** (m) A fried fresh tortilla stuffed with black beans and topped with shredded chicken or turkey and lettuce.

Periférico (sp) A big city peripheral road.

Plaza de Toros (bull ring) Major cities in Spain and Latin America have amphitheater sized bull rings known as *Plaza de Toros* where scheduled bullfights, usually six in a series, pit a swordsmen against a bull; many area variations exist. Small villages erect wooden scaffolding amphitheaters for seasonal festivals around Mexico.

Poc chuc (m) Thinly sliced pork marinated in the juice of sour orange and grilled over charcoal. It is served with a red onion relish, tomato sauce, black bean soup, comatose level hot habanero sauce, and fresh hand made tortillas.

Pool kan-es (m) Deep fried cakes of masa (corn dough) filled with *ibes*, a white lima bean, toasted ground squash seeds and chives.

Potaje de Lenteja (sp) This is a lentil stew with a variety of meats and vegetables.

Pozol (sp) Pozol is made by fermenting corn dough, which is rolled into balls. The drink is made by soaking the dough in water and adding chili, honey or sugar. In some places, chocolate is added.

Puchero (sp) A meat and vegetable stew traditionally served on Sunday in Yucatán.

Retablo (sp) An altarpiece of carved and painted wood that is usually gilded and displays religious paintings, relief carvings, and sculpted figures.

Sacbe (m) Sacbeob (plural of sacbe) Smooth, straight and nearly level white surfaced and plastered raised pedestrian roadways linking important Mayan sites. Not to be confused with "camino blanco" a limestone gravel surfaced road usually of Spanish origins.

Salbute (sp) A fresh tortilla fried in lard or oil until puffed and golden, then topped with layers of shredded chicken or turkey, lettuce or cabbage, red pickled onion, and topped with a sliced tomato.

Si Kil Pac (m) This is a flavorful nutritious Mayan dish of dried ground squash seeds mixed with diced tomatoes, habanero chili, onions, sour orange, and cilantro. It is served cold, and eaten with tortillas chips.

Suero (sp) A drink or powder used to replace bodily electrolytes. It is available at all pharmacies in Mexico.

Taller de Bordado (sp) A factory or workshop where embroidered clothing are made.

Toh (m) Name for the mot-mot bird. In Spanish it is *pájaro relojero*. This bird has a long pendulum type tail.

Topes (sp) Speed bumps used to slow road traffic. In Mexico they take many different forms. On coastal roads large ropes are used as *topes*.

Tortillaria (sp) A shop that sells fresh hot tortillas. In Yucatán they are of corn and produced by machine.

Triciclo (sp) In Yucatán it is a cargo cart coupled to a pusher bicycle that may be adapted to a variety of uses, the most common in villages being a tricycle taxi (*tricitaxi*).

Tunkul (m) Ceremonial log drum.

Vigas (sp) Ceiling beams made of wood in colonial times and today are made of pre-stressed cement beams.

Ya mero... no tarda mucho...falta poco! (sp) Almost there, not much longer, only lacking a little.

Yucatec Maya referring to the Mayan language spoken on the Yucatán Peninsula, distinctly different than that of Guatemala or Chiapas.

Zapote aka **sapote** (sp) Sapodilla is a fruit native to southern Mexico. The sap from the *zapote* trees is harvested for its high latex content and is called *chicle* and used in making chewing gum. The wood of the zapote tree is deep brown in color, very dense and hard. It is durable with exceptional resistance to decay. The ancient Maya used it in place of stone for headers in the doorways of their temples.

Zócalo (sp) Public square, main plaza or park.

190

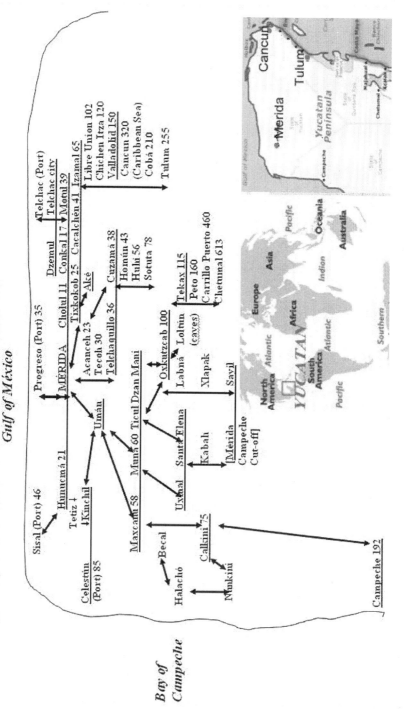

Mérida area map: ↑ North; Not to scale, numbers = distances in kilometers from Mérida

Gulf of México

Telchac (Port)
Telchac city
Dzemul Conkal 17 Motul 39
Progreso (Port) 35
Cholul 11 Tixkokob 25 Cacalchen 41 Izamal 65
MÉRIDA
Acanceh 23 Alcé
Tecoh 30 Cuzamá 38
Telchaquillo 36 Homún 43
Hunucmá 21 Huhí 56
Tetiz ↓ Sotuta 78
↓Kinchil
Umán
Libre Unión 102
Chichen Itzá 120
Valladolid 150
Cancún 320
(Caribbean Sea)
Cobá 210
Tulum 255

Sisal (Port) 46

Oxkutzcab 100
Loltún
(caves)
Tekax 115
Peto 160
Carrillo Puerto 460
Chetumal 613

Muná 60 Ticul Dzan Maní
Labná
Xlapak
Sayil

Santa Elena
Kabah
Uxmal
[Mérida
Campeche
Cut-off]

Maxcanú 58
Celestún
(Port) 85

Becal
Halachó
Nunkiní
Calkiní 75

Campeche 192

*Bay of
Campeche*

Resource Guide

Select Bibliography

This is a list of books that inspired us in our travels and exploration of the Yucatán and led us to the places that tourists miss most.

Ambivalent Conquests by Inga Clendinnen

Here and There in Yucatan **by** Alice Dixon

Identifying Villa Carlota: German Settlements in Yucatan, México, During the Second Empire (1864-1867) by Alma Judith Durán-Merk

Incidents of Travel in Yucatan by John L. Stephens

Life in Mexico by Madame (Frances Erskine Inglis) Calderón de la Barca, 1843

Mayan Missions by Richard and Rosalind Perry

Magic Yucatan by Lilo Linke

Six Months in Mexico by Nellie Bly, 1888

The American Egypt: A Record of Travel in Yucatan by Channing Arnold and Frederick J. Tabor Frost

The Caste War of Yucatan by Nelson A. Reed

The Cult of the Holy Cross by Charlotte Zimmerman

The Final Report by Michael Coe

The Folk-Lore of Yucatan by Daniel G. Brinton

The Maya Indians of Southern Yucatan and Northern British Honduras by Thomas Gann, 1908

The Maya by Michael Coe

The Lost World of Quintana Roo by Michel Peissel 1958

The True History of Chocolate by Sophie and Michael Coe

Time Among The Maya by Ronald Wright

Under the Waters of Mexico by Pablo Bush Romero

Yucatan: A World Apart by Edward H. Mosley and Edward D. Terry

Yucatan for Travelers – Side Trips: Valladolid to Tulum by John M. Grimsrud

A Yucatan Kitchen by Loretta Miller

Publications

Yucatan Today: Free monthly tourist guide magazine with excellent maps and tourist related information. It is available at hotels, restaurants, and information centers in Yucatán. Consult their website for the up-to-date information on festivals and events in Yucatán: http://yucatantoday.com

Bicycle tours

Bike Mexico with Basil and Alix; exceptional Yucatán tours plus western México. www.bikemexico.com

MexiGo in downtown Valladolid offers guided bicycle day tours + bike rentals   http://mexigotours.com

Helpful web sites

The author's websites and blogs:
www.bicycleyucatan.com
http://bingsbuzz.blogspot.com
www.bicycleyucatan.blogspot.com

Yucatán is the place to relax; you don't have to rush here. Take the time to enjoy a good book, not just read it.

Index

Books by John M. Grimsrud
The *Travel of Dursmirg* series ©2012 is in four volumes:
Sailing Beyond Lake Superior, *Travels of Dursmirg*, Vol. 1

This adventure story began as an idea and unfolded into a dream come true.

An obsession of escape materialized in 1972 with the building and launching of the dreamboat, *Dursmirg*.

John and Jane went over the horizon and out to sea on their adventurous voyage.

From Duluth-Superior, they crossed the Great Lakes to New York City. Snow turned them south. It was an enchanting journey, and in more than one place they felt tempted to stay. But there was always the thought of Florida driving them on.

They arrived in fairyland. Destiny planted them in St. Augustine.

This story relates the exciting happenings and action-packed personalities that forever altered their lives and changed its course.

Sailing the Sea Islands, *Travels of Dursmirg*, Volume 2

On Thanksgiving Day, 1972, they anchored at Daufuskie Island, South Carolina, their first taste of this enchanted land. The beautiful islands tempted them to stay, but Florida was beckoning. They pressed on south through Georgia to Florida, which was the culmination of a five year plan.

On May 22, 1973, after spending a glorious winter in St. Augustine, Florida, they pulled their anchor and headed north.

Now they would be returning with the time to enjoy life to the fullest. This wonderful new world that awaited them was filled with dazzling surprises.

Sailing the Sea Islands is about pristine beaches, secluded anchorages, fun loving people, fishing adventures, and seafood experiences spiced with delectable southern cooking.

Jane and John had been neophytes when it came to salt water fishing; they had a lot to learn and would discover the local tricks for living out of the sea.

Sailing the Florida Keys, *Travels of Dursmirg*, Volume 3

"We are going where the wind blows, when the spirit moves us, and the price is right." These were the driving forces that would be fulfilled beyond their wildest expectations.

Using St. Augustine, Florida, as a home base, winter sailing sojourns south always included the Indian River where lifelong friendships were cemented, bountiful seafood harvested, and anchorages were a slice of paradise.

Biscayne Bay was a cruising sail boater's dream come true with bountiful seafood, neat anchorages, and magical Miami there when your desires were tempted.

Dinner Key, Coconut Grove and Miami were all pulsating with an endless array or interesting things to do. Marvelous Cuban restaurants, back to the earth sun seekers, and salty sailors all added to the flavor.

Sailing the Florida Keys proved to be the best sailing, fishing, and exploring to be found anywhere.

Sailing to St. Augustine: Travels of Dursmirg, Volume 4

In this final book of the *Travels of Dursmirg* series, John and Jane step into the world of St. Augustine and meet the people, some of them rogues and social misfits, who made their time in St. Augustine a one-of-a-kind experience.

This story relates the action-packed events and exciting personalities that forever altered their lives and changed its course in St. Augustine, a place caught in the cross-hairs of time.

Yucatan for Travelers - Side Trips: Valladolid to Tulum
©2013

Valladolid is an excellently located colonial city steeped in history. Half way from Mérida, Cancun and Tulum, a diversity of spectacular side trips abound. The finest Mayan temples are nearby. This is the very best of tropical bird watching country.

For the armchair traveler and people that have been to Yucatán before and think that they have seen and done everything, *Yucatan for Travelers - Side Trips: Valladolid to Tulum* will open the door to special places not presented in tours or guided excursions. This isn't just a guide book but an idea book not made to compete with guidebooks like Lonely Planet or Moon Guide. It is made to complement them.

This book gives you a glimpse of some of Yucatan that tourists miss most. For an adventure that takes you out of the mainstream to explore some of this peaceful, quiet and fascinating world, follow in the author's path to the places without trinket shops and tour buses.

About the Author

John M. Grimsrud lives with his wife Jane in Mérida, Yucatán, in an ecologically friendly home of his own design. He has been biking, photographing, exploring, and writing about the Yucatán for over twenty-five years.

Made in the USA
Lexington, KY
07 April 2013